By Professor Ramanadham – A Select List

Public Enterprise in Britain (Frank Cass, London, 1959).

Problems of Public Enterprise (Quadrangle, Chicago)

The Structure of Public Enterprise in India
(Asia Publishing House, New York, 1961)

The Finances of Public Enterprises
(Asia Publishing House, New York, 1963)

Control of Public Enterprises in India
(Asia Publishing House, New York, 1964).

The Structure of the British Electricity Supply Industry
(Kamath, Mangalore, 1954).

The Yugoslav Enterprise (ICPE, Ljubljana, 1982).

Parliament and Public Enterprise (ICPE, Ljubljana, 1982)
(With Professor Yash Ghai).

*Organization, Management and Supervision of Public Enterprise
in Developing Countries* (United Nations, 1974).

The Nature of Public Enterprise
(Croom Helm, London, 1984)

Studies in Public Enterprise
(Frank Cass, London, 1987)

Books edited

Pricing and Investment in Public Enterprise
(Oxford IBH, 1974).

*Joint Ventures and Public Enterprises
in Developing Countries* (ICPE, Ljubljana, 1980).

Public Enterprise and the Developing World
(Croom Helm, London, 1984).

Public Enterprise: Studies in Organisational Structure
(Frank Cass, London, 1986).

STUDIES IN PUBLIC ENTERPRISE

From Evaluation to Privatisation

V.V. RAMANADHAM
London Business School

FRANK CASS

HD
3850
. R35
1987

First published 1987 in Great Britain by
FRANK CASS AND COMPANY LIMITED
Gainsborough House, 11 Gainsborough Road,
London, E11 1RS, England

and in the United States of America by
FRANK CASS AND COMPANY LIMITED
c/o Biblio Distribution Centre
81 Adams Drive, P.O. Box 327, Totowa, N.J. 07511

British Library Cataloguing in Publication Data

Ramanadham, V.V.
    Studies in public enterprise: from evaluation
    to privatisation
    1. Government ownership
    I. Title
338.6   HD3850

ISBN 0-7146-3267-8

Library of Congress Cataloging-in-Publication Data

Ramanadham, V. V. (Venkata Vemuri), 1920-
    Studies in public enterprise.

    Includes index.
    1. Government business enterprises--Case studies.
I. Title.
HD3850R35   1986   351.009'2   86-991
ISBN 0-7146-3267-8

Printed and bound in Great Britain by
A. Wheaton & Co. Ltd, Exeter

To
KRISHNA, LEELA AND SASANKA
of whom I am proud

TABLES

FIGURES

APPENDICES

CONTENTS

PREFACE

This book contains studies on some important aspects of public enterprise, based on the experience of a wide spectrum of developed and developing countries. "Public Enterprise and Evaluation" seeks to introduce some fundamental ideas on the concept of evaluation at four levels, deals with evaluation as a system and succinctly reviews the experience of the United Kingdom, Argentina, Malaysia, Pakistan, Nepal and India. "Capital Structures of Public Enterprises" brings out the economic issues that are implicit in the arrangements of capitalisation in vogue in the public enterprise sector. "Public Enterprise and the Public Exchequer" is an in-depth analytical study of certain aspects of the budget link of public enterprises and shows how this has not yet been adequately realised. And "Privatisation in the African Context" deals with the concept of privatisation, now coming into prominence, and presents a nondoctrinaire review of the problems it raises.

These studies have all been prepared in the course of my researches while at the London Business School in 1982–83, in response to invitations to deliver lectures. Much of the material contained in the study on Evaluation forms part of my Lal Bahadur Shastri Memorial Lecture at New Delhi, India. The second study – on Capital Structures – was delivered as the Fifth Shoaib Memorial Lecture at Karachi, Pakistan. The third is based on the Jalagam Vengal Rao Endowment Lecture at Tirupati, India. The "Privatisation" paper was prepared for the Conference on "State Shrinking: A Comparative Inquiry into Privatisation" at Austin, USA. It will appear in a book bearing that title.

I express my thanks to Mr T.L. Sankar, Director, Institute of Public Enterprise, India; Mr Riyaz Bokhari, Chairman, Institute of Cost and Management Accountants of Pakistan; Professor M.V. Rama Sarma, Vice-Chancellor, S.V. University, India, and Professor William Glade, Director, Institute of Latin American

Studies, University of Texas, Austin, for their invitations which prompted me to undertake these studies, and for their kind consent to let me publish the material in the form of this book.

Acknowledgements are due to a number of professional friends in many countries, with whom I had illuminating discussions in the conduct of these studies. Further I received from many of them comments on the first drafts, which immensely helped me in improving the accuracy and clarity of presentation. May I mention, in particular, Professor David Chambers, Professor John Heath, Mr Nick Woodward, Mr George Ronson, Mr T.U. Burgner, Sir D.N. Chester, Professor Yash Ghai, Professor Maurice Garner, Dr A.M.H. Bennett – from the United Kingdom; Mr Riyaz Bokhari, Mr A. Raouf (Auditor General), Major Gen. (Retd.) Syed Ali Nawab – from Pakistan; Dr R. Rajagopalan, Mr S. Rangarajan, Mr T.M.C. Menon, Professor Laxmi Narain – from India; Mr L.B. Shrestha, Mr L. Dixit, Mr A. Rana – from Nepal; Dr Horacio Boneo from Argentina; and Mr A. Premchand from the International Monetary Fund. I convey my thanks to them all.

Professor V.V. Ramanadham
London Business School

PART ONE

Public Enterprise and Evaluation

INTRODUCTION

The aim of this study is to present evaluation in the context of public enterprise in analytical terms and as a system, employing global experience for illustrative purposes.

Evaluation, as conceived here, has a broad conceptual range. It connotes evaluation of the performance of the managers, evaluation of the performance of the enterprise inclusive of governmental involvement in it, evaluation of the compatibility of the enterprise operations with social and macro interests, and evaluation of the institutional merits of the enterprise as an entity in the national economy.

The need to evolve evaluation on such a broad basis arises from the heavy stakes that many countries, especially the developing economies, have in the institution of public enterprise.

Evaluation as a system has four major components: the concept of evaluation, the substantive content of evaluation, the requisites of evaluation, and the agencies of evaluation. These call for precise interlinking. There are elements of a jigsaw puzzle here. Our aim should be to maximise systemic coherence in bringing these together or to minimise systemic incoherence. This is the idea pursued in the study.

Let me signpost the study. The four components of the system will be discussed in order, bringing out the interrelationships as we go. Towards the end there will be reviews of the system as it exists in selected countries from different regions – the United Kingdom (UK), Argentina, Malaysia, Nepal, Pakistan and India.

1

The Concept of Evaluation

The first step in an analysis of evaluation in the context of public enterprise is to be clear on the concept of evaluation. There is a wide diversity of understanding in this respect. At one extreme it is equated with the ensuring of accountability on the part of the managers entrusted with the operations of a public enterprise, as may be gleaned from the (UK) Industry and Trade Committee's reference to "the Government's belief that a public sector body which gains a considerable proportion of its revenue from monopoly activities should be properly accountable for the way in which it uses its monopoly power."[1]

Similar is the import of the UK Government's decision, cited in the CAG's Memorandum, that "industries not fully exposed to competition should be subjected to regular external efficiency audit."[2]

A few other illustrations of a relatively restrictive understanding of the evaluation concept are worth citing from the British scene. The Monopolies and Mergers Commission referred to the Audit Department of the National Coal Board as monitoring "the efficiency of the NCB's activities."[3]

The (UK) Transport Committee termed the work of the Serpell Committee on Railway Finances as "in essence, a management and efficiency audit,"[4] and saw in it an opportunity for the Department of Trade to obtain "an independent assessment of the Board's practices in these areas."

The idea of a "customer audit" was advanced by the (UK) Post Office Users' National Council. It would be "a means of monitoring whether the customer is getting value for money," and it would be "a continuing review of the Post Office's performance."[5]

Emphasis on the idea of the managers performing well and of assuring the government of this can also be inferred from the conclusions of the National Economic Development Office's studies in 1976. They commented on the absence of an "external audit mechanism," "which might provide reassurance to Government and Parliament about the effectiveness of management organisation and procedures within the industry."[6]

The point for emphasis is not that the quest for evaluation implicit in these citations is wrong: far from it, indeed. It has a limited connotation and represents no more than a minimal element of what evaluation in the context of public enterprise ought to imply.

THE ANALOGY OF CONCENTRICITY

Let me develop this theme by introducing the analogy of concentricity. As shown in the following diagram (Figure 1), four levels of evaluation can be distinguished. A relates to the evaluation of the managers, B to the evaluation of the enterprise as a whole, C to the evaluation of the compatibility of the enterprise results with social interests, and D to the evaluation of the comparative advantage of the public enterprise.

FIGURE 1

FOUR LEVELS OF EVALUATION

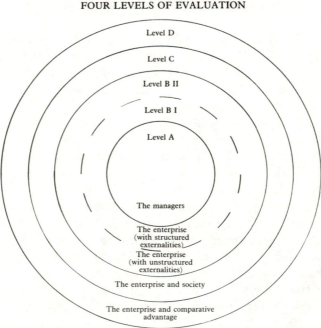

The simplest and minimal level is that of evaluating the managers, inclusive of the board level. Very often this is the sense in which the concept is understood. It is in that way that the government can place itself on the side of the evaluator. The idea that the managers are to be accountable for the resources and functions entrusted to them as well as the familiar term of "management audit" is traceable to this context.

There is nothing wrong about this, as already suggested. It is just not enough, even if their accountability is understood in the positive sense of maximal behaviour in the use of resources. We now go to the B–level. The performance of the managers (by whatever criteria we look at it) is the end result not merely of their own capability but of all the impacts on their behaviour from government interventions. These are of no small significance in shaping not only the final results of enterprise operations but even what appear to be managerial strategies and logistics which constitute the substance of what is sought to be evaluated at the A–level.

A few illustrations may be cited from the UK scene.

> The scrutiny by the Department of Industry of the Post Office's activities is too detailed and too intrusive for a body which is supposed to be a commercial enterprise.

(Fifth Report from the Industry and Trade Committee (Session 1981–82) *The Post Office* (London, 1982), p. ix.)

> We feel bound to conclude that the Board could have had lower costs in recent years if it had been free to pursue the objective of cost reduction by every means possible ...
>
> The Board's procurement costs could have been lower. This arises not from lack of efficiency in use of its existing resources, but from concern on its own or the Government's part for the interests of the major suppliers.

(The Monopoly and Mergers Commission, *Central Electricity Generating Board* (London 1981), pp. 291–2.)

> The Secretary of State's decision "to retain five sites was essentially a political rather than an economic decision .... In our view the decision is extremely costly."

(Second Report from the Industry and Trade Committee (Session

1982–83), *The British Steel Corporation's Prospects* (London, 1983), pp. xi–xii.)

Apart from widening the concept of evaluation, the B–level already has a purport for who should evaluate and what that agency should seek to evaluate. Briefly, the agency has to be other than the sponsoring department of the government, and the range of evaluation has to cover the role of the government itself in the working of the enterprise. That this does not happen may be evidenced from a comment such as the following by David Chambers: "In the case of UK nationalised industries, official discussion has drawn the system boundaries very narrowly. The system to be managed is taken as the Nationalised Industry itself, not the larger configuration of the Industry, its sponsoring Ministry and the Treasury Division."[7]

Perhaps it is useful to distinguish between two parts of the extra–enterprise role in enterprise performance: the interventions built into formal structures, e.g., the board of directors, the issue of directives, and the established procedures of governmental communication with the enterprises; and the impacts of an informal, political and ad hoc nature. The latter may be derived from civil servants (e.g., in the course of budget discussions), from ministers (e.g., in informal meetings, if not lunches), from members of parliament (e.g., through criticism voiced in and out of the House), and from political parties (in diverse ways). These influences are difficult to establish,[8] so are their impacts on performance difficult to evaluate. Yet they are too real to overlook. They may be distinguished in the B II circle, while the "structured" interventions go into the B I circle.

At stage C the concept of evaluation begins to be marked by a distinctive twist. The emphasis here is not on how well or ill the managers and any others who have had a role in influencing managerial behaviour performed. The aim is to evaluate what purport the enterprise results have to society.[9] The point of substance is how the results agree with the interests of society. That the latter have probably not been set out in clear terms is surely a limitation on the enterprise consciously aiming to achieve a specific spectrum of results. What assumes importance at this stage of the evaluation spiral is how society reacts to whatever has been achieved by the enterprise. If one remembers that in a mixed economy, a public enterprise carries a distinctive set of macro obligations, the case for this level of evaluation can be easily appreciated. (How logically the interests of society can be identified in this connection is another question, difficult but necessary to confront, the more so in a developing country.)

Finally we come to stage D, where evaluation has to cover an adjudication of the comparative advantage of a public enterprise in respect of given sectoral operations. Far from being an inquisition into who, if at all, is to be blamed and for what, this is an approach quite essential to progress; for it allows, if not prompts, the government to gain knowledge on whether it is worth continuing with a given enterprise in the public sector, taking into account "current" market conditions and aspects of social preferences, or whether any changes in its entrepreneurial and ownership structure appear to be commendable. At the minimum, the issue can be simply this: are structural and operating changes necessary, despite continued public ownership, in order that the enterprise retains its comparative advantage? At the other end the question is whether it has sustained such a loss of comparative advantage that privatisation can be beneficial to the economy. Some rethinking on these lines is currently in progress in several developing countries, for example, Peru,[10] Sri Lanka, Sudan[11] and Kenya. For instance, in Kenya the Working Party on Government Expenditures in 1982 suggested that government participation in enterprises had, in several cases, reached the point where it was "inhibiting rather than providing development by Kenyans themselves." They recommended a review so as to establish, among other things, enterprises "whose functions would be more efficiently performed by the private sector."[12] These views have relevance to our point under discussion, in that they underline the importance of evaluation of the D type. Were this to be in continuous progress, the implementation of policies of divestiture and other forms of privatisation could be as prompt as desired.

Let us draw some conclusions from this part of our analysis.

First, each level of evaluation implies a distinctive purpose of such evaluation. Unfortunately there has been greater concern in most countries on the question of who evaluates than on the precise purpose of evaluation. The UK experience is somewhat refreshing; but even there the point reached is that of verifying how an enterprise "is measuring up to its objectives," and the objectives are elaborated in terms of "the main points in the corporate plan, ... the financial target, ... the cash limit, ... suitable aims in terms of performance and service, ... and any general or specific directions given to it."[13] This approach, no doubt, satisfies certain requisites of internal consistency of evaluation as a system, as will be clear from the following sections. What it does not satisfy is the full range of the concept of evaluation, from levels A to D; nor does the question of social efficiency of a public enterprise, corresponding to levels C and D, receive clear recognition. Such a gap has material consequences for a developing country which one day may wake up either to be surprised by the socio-economic consequences of a given enterprise's operations or to rush to schemes of privatisation.

Second, the different levels of evaluation indicated in the figure are not equally important in respect of all enterprises or in all countries. For instance, an enterprise taken over on mere grounds of mismanagement deserves essentially the A–level evaluation. At the other extreme an electricity enterprise calls for the C–level and a consumer goods unit, in due course, for the D–level.

Third, the different levels of evaluation are not mutually exclusive. The inter-connections are substantial indeed. For example, any review of the managers' performance has to make full provision for the managerial impacts traceable to external forces. How conclusively this can be done is, in fact, a major technical problem. The problem gets complicated as we need to discover not only the implications of external influences for the operating decisions by the managers but also the consequences, which may be construed, of investment constraints and locational restrictions traceable to governmental determinations. Interesting examples are provided by the Post Office and British Steel Corporation in the UK.[14]

When we are at levels C and D, i.e., when we evaluate what a public enterprise means to society and what its comparative advantage currently is, we need to make a sub-evaluation of whether the data on the managers' performance (analogous to level A) and the enterprise performance (analogous to level B) are good enough as a basis. We ought not to rush to conclusions at the C and D levels without examining whether the findings relating to the A and B levels reveal circumstances that can be remedied so materially that comparative advantage once again accumulates in favour of the enterprise and of its continued existence in the public sector. The solutions needed may perhaps consist of a reform in the managerial practices (or even personnel) and in the government's procedures of managerial and directoral involvement, rather than anything more radical or structural. In other words, the systemic inter-relationships between the A–and–B levels and the C–and–D levels need to be kept in mind.

Fourth, evaluation in the context of public enterprise is basic-ally a part of the development strategy in a developing country. It has a connotation that greatly transcends the performance of the managers of a given enterprise. The end question that one has to face is how the results of an enterprise – as it has operated or can be made to operate – impact on the development interests of the nation; and what changes may be desirable in its entrepreneurial and organisational structure in order that it can constitute a more effective instrument of development. The validity of such con-siderations is greater in a developing country than in a developed country; and dubious answers can have more serious consequen-ces as well. It is, therefore, important for governments of develop-ing countries to approach evaluation in its broad context of deve-lopment. It is from this angle that this study is entitled "Public Enterprise and Evaluation," attaching more than semantic signifi-cance to the title in contradistinction to the more familiar term "evaluation of public enterprise."

Fifth, evaluation has to be conceived of as a system, of which the A, B, C and D levels are parts. Experience suggests, on the other hand, that it is bits of performance or operating results of an enterprise that are made the subject matter of a review, whatever the term used to describe the review. The Inquiries by Tribunals in Nigeria in the 1960s are an example; they highlighted many managerial malpractices. The (UK) Monopolies and Mergers Commission's enquiry relating to the London Electricity Board in 1983 was confined to its retailing of electrical appliances and any monopoly and deficit implications of the practices. The Serpell Committee (in the UK) was appointed in 1982 "to examine the finances" of British Railways Board and "to report on options . . . designed to secure improved financial results in an efficiently run railway in Great Britain over the next 20 years."

And then there are, in many countries, extended audits con-ducted by the Auditor General. The findings emerging from such reviews are unlikely to provide a firm basis for evaluation in the comprehensive sense in which the concept is presented here. It seems, therefore, to be a first requirement for governments to evaluate the arrangements made in the name of, or towards achieving, evaluation in the context of public enterprise. Two good results can follow. This helps in identifying how near to (or far from) the total concept of evaluation specific evaluation measures stand and keeps us from rushing to evaluational conclusions. Second, it can stimulate the evolution of a comprehensive system of evaluation, of which the existing practices may be consciously deemed as contributory bits.

LEVEL AND CONTENT

We shall next look at the systemic inter relationships between the level (or purpose) of evaluation and the substantive content of evaluation.

Level A

Briefly, it is the performance of the managers that is sought to be evaluated at this level. The results achieved by them have to be evaluated in the context of the options of behaviour open to them. The options are under two categories of constraints: first, the investment and allied decisions taken by past managements or by, or at the instance of, the government; and second, current managerial interventions from external sources. Assuming that the managers had no way of freeing themselves from the impacts of these constraints, we would find it meaningful to make an appraisal of their performance subject to these qualifications, bearing in mind that our focus should be on the balance of risks – not the successes only – achieved in the course of their decisional matrix. For instance, within the constraints of external interventions, have they done their best in performance budgeting, capital budgeting, corporate planning, management development etc.? The appraisal may adopt a two-pronged approach:

(i)   Have the managers satisfied the criteria or objectives or targets set, if any? This approximates to the UK White Paper's idea of "how well" the enterprise was "measuring to its objectives."[15]

(ii) Where the objectives or targets have not been set in sufficiently meaningful terms from the standpoint of managerial behaviour, the question would be: have they done as well as they could be expected to perform? Not an easy task, this part of the appraisal can gain from a review of the results of the enterprise over a period, from a review of its results as against those of "like" enterprises, and from a constructive speculation of what managers "in the circumstances" could possibly do. A recent illustration may be drawn from the (UK) MMC's enquiry of the Yorkshire Electricity Board, in which it concluded, in respect of its operational and administrative costs: "We believe the organisation should set itself the aim of doing significantly better than this."[16]

The purpose of evaluation at this stage has to be wide enough to cover the following:

(i) It may suggest changes in managerial personnel, managerial structure or managerial practices so as to promote improved results.

(ii) It may suggest the advisability of effecting changes in objectives and targets – especially when these are far exceeded or under-realised[17] or when these are internally set by the management itself without the government's involvement in the exercise.

(iii) It may prompt thought on ways of dealing with the constraint factors impinging on managerial performance.

Level B

The subject for evaluation at this level is the overall performance of the enterprise. We have to be clear about the meaning of this term. In so far as the bare end results achieved, Level A has already dealt with the question – *but* subject to certain qualifications. Now we go into the qualifications and address the question of external (mainly government) interventions in the processes of decision and managerial operations. It is not always easy to single these out neatly; for some of the interventions occur through board decisions which, in one sense, are an "internal" prerogative of an autonomous enterprise, but which in de facto terms can be an inbuilt governmental intervention. Subject to this difficulty, the problem may be categorised under two heads:

(i) Has the system of governmental interventions, inclusive of the procedures, been maximal in effects? These occur, at the minimum, as a routine sequel to the various duties placed by the Acts on the ministries in the context of public enterprise operations.[18]

A few gentle comments on "the effectiveness of the monitoring and controlling operations of the sponsor Departments of Nationalised Industries" are available in the Memorandum of the Comptroller and Auditor General submitted to the (UK) Committee of Public Accounts. Earlier instances from the UK can be drawn from the Report of the Select Committee on Nationalised Industries on the Capital Investment Procedures[19] which contained significant comments that bordered on evaluating the nature of the governmental role in the working of public enterprises.

(ii) Has the government decided on the best of the options open to it in realising any given macro objectives through the instrumentality of a public enterprise? These range widely over investment, prices, location, closures, employment and so on. If, for instance, an investment control has been exercised, the questions to examine would be: (1) whether the substance of the control has been in the macro interest, (2) whether that could have been better realised in any other way than through an investment control measure, and (3) whether the procedure of the control measure as adopted has been the most conducive to the expected results. Price controls are another instance that lends clarity to the nature of questions raised here: have they been in the macro interest, would other measures have been more effective, and have the procedures of control been most fruitful?

An end result of evaluation at the B–level is to streamline the external impacts on public enterprise operations in such a way as to maximise their value for the economy. This has relevance to the question of agency of evaluation. Obviously it cannot be the ministries themselves. The Comptroller and Auditor General and Parliamentary Committees can be of help, by virtue of their constitutional status and privilege of seeking the necessary kind of information "internal" to government.

An evaluation that does not cover the B–level is bound to be of limited value. At one extreme, its consequences may consist of an over-emphasis on managerial under-performance, even as government interventions continue to manifest themselves in an amateurish manner.

Level C

At this level we move away from evaluation in terms of the actors. Independently of that angle, we address the question as to how society views the results of the working a public enterprise. It is somewhat implicit in the earlier questions of whether the managers met their targets and the ministries monitored them effectively.

The results may be evaluated under the two broad heads of financial returns and social returns. (Physical indicators concerning output, employment, technology, etc. may be suitably incorporated under these two heads, as far as possible.) The evaluation essentially relates to the way in which the "public" and the "enterprise" elements underlying the very concept of public enterprise have been synthesised. Without going into the details of the synthesis,[20] we may sum up the issues as follows:

(i)   How satisfactorily are the results, especially under the head of social returns, identified and quantified?
(ii) What weights are attached to those results and how are the social returns weighted, individually or together, as against the financial returns?

To these conceptual and computational problems we may add the question of what sanctity or authority attaches to the value judgements implicit in this whole area.

One result of the C–level evaluation is to prompt reforms in the working of a given enterprise so as to conduce to more socially acceptable patterns of results than have been realised. At the minimum it is to show the way for the right public interventions calculated to stop or minimise results not desired or results that are positively undesirable – for example, operations that aggravate foreign control in a sector or pricing that subsidises rich consumers or a technology that wastefully emphasises capital rather than labour as an input. It follows that the agency to which the task of evaluation is assigned should be provided with guidelines on the computational and value–judgement aspects and that its composition should be so determined as to facilitate a satisfactory social appraisal. Such an appraisal can be a basis for the government or Parliament to design changes in the results to be expected from an enterprise.

Level D

Here we go a step further than at Level C, in that the evaluation is expected to show whether a given enterprise has experienced any change in its comparative advantage. The problem arises, again, of making a judgement taking together the financial and social returns. Where in both respects the situation is favourable or unfavourable in comparison with an earlier time horizon or a private enterprise, the conclusion can be somewhat easy. But where the trends under the two heads are different, we face the basic problem of how to weigh one against the other.

Consistent with the result of evaluation at this level, the agency should include strong non-official expertise. It is particularly important that in developing countries it should meticulously examine policy options short of denationalisation; for denationalisation might be difficult to implement in their circumstances of capital markets. In countries more or less ideologically oriented to a dominant or overwhelming public enterprise sector, it is the options other than denationalisation that alone will be of practical relevance (see Part IV for a further discussion of this point.) Hence the D–level evaluation should concentrate on the nature of marketisation plausible within the structure of the national economy.

Two points, in conclusion. First, the levels A to D are not necessarily transitive. A and B are the most inter-related; while C and D can be undertaken even apart from A and B.

Second, in most countries even the A–level of evaluation is not satisfactorily undertaken yet. This does not negate the need, however, for their quest for a conceptually sound and comprehensive system covering all the levels from A to D. The need is the greatest in developing countries.

2

The Substance: the Typological Approach

As we move to the second of the systemic aspects of evaluation, viz., the substance, we soon discover that some enterprises are relatively easy and some rather complex to evaluate. This is due to the nature of their economic characteristics. The most important of these are worth noting so that the requisite focus may be placed on identifying the substantive elements of each characteristic which call for special attention on the part of the evaluating agency.

It is from this angle that a typology of enterprise characteristics is presented below (Table 1). They are not claimed to be exhaustive. However, they cover the major area under reference; besides, though they appear to be economic and organisational, they can accommodate several other features associated with the working of enterprises.

It may be noted that the characteristics denoted in the Table are not mutually exclusive.

TABLE 1

TYPOLOGY OF PUBLIC ENTERPRISE CHARACTERISTICS

Characteristic (1)	*Some annotation* (2)
1. Organisation structure	*Holding complex*/unitary/joint venture/ sectoral/multi-sectoral/*integration*
2. Size	*Large*/small
3. Product mix	Single/*multi-product*
4. Capital – output/labour ratio	*High*/low
5. R & D	*Sophisticated*/simple
6. Location	Single/*dispersed*/*backward-region*
7. Monopoly	*High*/low
8. Market composition	*Public-sector oriented*/not so
9. Externalities	*Significant*/low – Infra-structural/public-utility
10. Financial viability	High/Bare/*Negative*
11. Special factors	*Significant*/nominal

An enterprise with an italicised characteristic presents greater complexity for evaluation than one without it. Where an enterprise bristles with many characteristics italicised, evaluation becomes difficult indeed.

We shall now examine the distinctive purport of each characteristic.

A. ORGANISATIONAL STRUCTURE

The term covers a variety of ideas, of which five are highlighted below.

(a) Where the enterprise is a *holding* complex, the questions which call for particular attention in the course of evaluation are as follows:

(i)   Is the systemic efficiency of management inhibited by over-centralisation and other incidentals of the holding–company organisation? And is the overall performance of the managers adversely affected in this process?

(ii)   Do cross-subsidisations exist – open or disguised: for example, in transfer–pricing, in procurement of capital, in designing cost/profit centres, and in allocating common costs? Do these complicate inferences from the results that the books of account present? Are meticulous adjustments in accounting and other areas needed so as to come up with reliable conclusions on the results of the individual components of the enterprise and of the enterprise itself – in the context of evaluation at any level, A to D?

(iii) If the holding complex operates in a single sector, it has a corresponding proneness to monopoly power, whereas if it is multi-sectoral in composition, this tendency may not be equally strong. (Further points regarding monopoly as a characteristic will be picked up under (G) below.)

(b) Where the enterprise represents an *integration* of processes – forward or backward – three questions demand attention in particular:

(i)   Transfer pricing as between the processes;

(ii)   Pricing decisions that might be having the effect of presenting unfair competition to other units engaged in some of the processes;

(iii) A rigorous scrutiny of the argument concerning economies of integration. For example, how balanced are the integrated processes in point of scale economies?

(c) Where the enterprise has a *monolithic* structure, questions concerning the efficiency of internal organisation merit evaluation. To cite a recent instance, the monolithic Nepal Electricity Corporation has so far remained heavily centralised in terms of managerial action. It is only now that some regionalisation below the level of the general manager is being contemplated. How effective the process turns out to be should be a point of interest in evaluation as applied to this enterprise.

(d) Another dimension of the organisational structure relates to the *ownership status* of the enterprise: where it is a joint venture, evaluation has to concern itself, among other things, with the following questions:

(i) Are the management (or directoral) arrangements such that they contribute to maximising capability? Or, is the government's share so unwieldy as to inhibit managerial efficiency?

(ii) Of special relevance to level C: does the joint venture have any unintended consequences in the realm of income distribution; and, if the jointness is with foreigners, does it operate as an unacceptable medium of foreign control over the national economy? In broad terms the question is whether private interests are exploiting public ownership to their advantage.

(e) A common feature of most public enterprises in developing countries is the absence of *management development* planning.[21] This should attract evaluatory attention especially in the case of complex organisations.

B. SIZE

The size of an enterprise has implications for its efficiency and performance. Evaluation exercises should be mindful of the following points:

(a) Is the largeness of an enterprise – and many enterprises in the public sector are large – really economical? The economies of scale need to be examined rigorously in view of the usually over-worked case for large sizes. In developing countries the case is sought to be strengthened on grounds of conservation of resources, including managerial resources, and of the needs of co-ordination. Redundancies in the supply structure are worth curbing, if they really prove wasteful over the long run.

(b) Are there elements of excess capacity? If they exist, their cost consequences as well as the appropriateness of managerial decisions in price-fixing call for scrutiny.

(c) A major question that evaluation agencies have to address is how, in circumstances probably unconducive to fundamental size reductions, the economy of operations can be maximised through internal reorganisations that emphasise the identification of the right operating levels, and cost and profit centres.

(d) Large size possibly implies cross-subsidisations. These have consequences for the consumers; also they can shelter inefficiency at certain points of production within the enterprise.

(e) It is possible that, in some cases, the enterprises are too small to be economical, e.g. at the state government level in India. Establishing factual evidence in this regard would be of utmost relevance to evaluation, not only at level A but at level D.

(f) With reference to a sector of activity whose growth potential is considerable, it should be a fit point for evaluation whether an existing enterprise should seek to expand or a new enterprise should be established and allowed entry in the field.

C. PRODUCT MIX

Three facets of the product mix may be highlighted.

(a) Does an enterprise sufficiently diversify its production structure so as to maximise the degree of utilisation of every resource input it has acquired and also to insure itself against risks of dependence on a single product market?

(b) Where the enterprise is engaged in marketing multiple products, does it practise cross-subsidisations? Do these have a social justification? And do they have (undesirable) impacts on competitors engaged in any of the products?

(c) If the product mix is technologically rather casual, e.g., as between postal and telecommunication services, how strong is the case for determining separate financial targets for the broadly distinct sections of its activity? Even if they are not determined, it has to be a part of the evaluation exercise to review the question.

D. CAPITAL OUTPUT/LABOUR RATIO

The most obvious remit for evaluation here is to examine the degree of utilisation of capital in terms of production and/or the input of labour. In countries where capital is relatively scarce and labour is plentiful, and where a significant proportion of capital investment comes from outside, the ratios of capital to output and labour assume particular significance. The value of reviewing these may be appreciated from the fact that, in many developing countries, public enterprises have tended to be capital-intensive[22] and under-utilised.[23] The ease of securing capital is a contributory factor. How far the situation is amenable to change should be a point of practical interest.

An equally interesting aspect would be the degree of substitutability as between capital and labour, so as to economise, wherever possible, the input of the more scarce factor. Of course a review of this has to be mindful of the long-term needs of technological efficiency, which ought not to be sacrificed in the name of appropriate technology.

E. R & D

It should be of special interest in evaluation to enquire into the record of an enterprise in R & D, technological innovation or technological absorption. This is all the more important in sectors where technological progress happens to be an important requisite of long-term competitiveness of the activity and where a public enterprise is considered by the government as a national vehicle of technological advancement. Also, where the pressures of the market are not too material and the degree of monopoly power is high, does the enterprise show sufficient dynamism in this managerial or growth area?

F. LOCATION

This, like certain other aspects of the original investment decision, has an impact on the economies of the enterprise. It can even be permanent. Appraising it would be of interest to almost all levels of evaluation, the more so in situations of deliberate location of an enterprise in an under-developed region: for example, a sugar mill where adequate supplies of cane are doubtful and a steel works where neither iron nor coal exists. Evaluation has to bring out the extent of social subsidisation that is implicit in such decisions, so that the most appropriate conclusions may be drawn on the performance of the enterprise and on the merits of seeking a given social end through the enterprise. Another aspect of the location issue is that several major public enterprises have widely dispersed plants – e.g., British Steel Corporation, Bharat Heavy Electricals Ltd. and Coal India Ltd. Apart from being large, they call for the attention of evaluation agencies to the following questions:

(a) Are locational decisions on production maximally oriented? That is, are additions to output realised from those plants and locations that are the most economical; are contractions, when necessary, effected in such a way that the least economical locations or plants will be the first to experience production cuts? Or, is output scheduling done without reference to costs of production and marketing and with an eye on keeping even inefficient units in commission?

(b) How local or national are the influences on industrial relations? Are wages geared to conditions of productivity and earnings prevalent at the plant level? Or, is every issue raised to the level of national determination? An interesting example of the local nature of the determining influences comes from Yugoslavia where practically every (small) basic organisation of associated labour is the level that counts most. The recent trend towards local plant influence on wage matters in British Steel is worth citing too. Contrast these with the almost national character of wage awards in the major industries of India.

G. MONOPOLY

This is among the usual but not invariable characteristics of many public enterprises. As such it will be purposeful for evaluation to concern itself with such questions as the following:

(a) Has monopoly power been exercised by an enterprise, with effects on size of output, quality and terms of supply, price, inter-consumer interests, innovation and growth?
(b) Is there any relationship between such effects and social preferences, if known?
(c) Have monopoly practices harboured inefficiency of any kind and at any level of enterprise operations?

Little wonder that these questions are so fundamental that about the most effective segment of the evaluation framework that exists in the UK consists of enquiries by the Monopolies and Mergers Commission (MMC) into the affairs of a nationalised industry on reference from the minister and in relation to the terms of reference. (More on this in Section 5.) Unfortunately few other countries including India present similar investigatory attention to public enterprise monopoly.

H. MARKET COMPOSITION

A closely related issue which merits the attention of evaluation agencies is the market composition of the enterprise. Where the customer composition is heavily dominated by government departments and/or public enterprises,[24] pricing practices can be a product of monopoly, monopsony or family-bargaining. The relevant cost conditions and surplus generation needs may not receive due attention.

I. EXTERNALITIES

These constitute one of the basic pillars of public enterprise as an institution. It is expected to internalise various kinds of preferences external to the enterprise. However, not every enterprise in the public sector is equally affected by them. The major problem in any evaluation is, therefore, to identify the exact social preferences to which an enterprise is exposed and then proceed to review their impacts on its operations as well as the accomplishments of the enterprise as against the public expectations. The technical questions that arise in this context are as follows:

(a) How real is the result achieved through enterprise operations, vis-a-vis the social preference in question?
(b) What is the extent of the deflection from the enterprise economics that internalisation of it has caused?
(c) How has the financial consequence of such internalisation been met by the enterprise? How has it been shifted to consumers, if at all?[25]
(d) Does the question of financial consequence, as claimed by the managers, contain elements of an alibi for any inefficiency on their side?

Certain categories of enterprises such as the public utilities and those operating in infrastructural fields are assumed to be highly potential of social returns, in terms of growth as well as social justice. Such enterprises should prompt the evaluation agencies to explore the above questions in particular.

J. FINANCIAL VIABILITY

There is a general feeling that an enterprise whose financial surplus is high is doing well and that an enterprise with poor financial returns is doing badly. Despite serious qualifications, governments have begun to feel concerned about deficits on the part of public enterprises; and the managers constantly suffer from a stigma. It will be a task of evaluation to probe situations of deficits with the object, among others, of distinguishing the causes that are beyond the control of the managers and those that can be attributed to them. Besides, the responsibility of directoral and managerial involvements on the part of the government has to be traced. The level of financial viability may trigger attention, no doubt; but the evaluation agency has to treat it as the end result of how the earlier mentioned characteristics of the enterprise have manifested themselves.

K. SPECIAL FACTORS

Under this head we refer to any characteristics of a special nature, which a given enterprise is marked by. For instance, it may have come into the public sector as a result of mismanagement or fraud on the part of erstwhile private managers; or it may have a long history of poor industrial relations; or it is a chronically sick unit taken over from the private sector. In such cases evaluation has to cover the special factors relevant to the enterprise.

Obviously an enterprise presents diverse degrees of complexity under the different heads of characteristics – a point illustrated by Table 2 in which two enterprises each from the UK, India, Kenya and Pakistan are entered. Symbol A denotes the utmost of complexity, and symbol C denotes the least complexity. B is an intermediate situation. It is interesting to see that British Railways Board has seven As as against the Mumias Sugar Co. which has as many as six Cs. (The symbolisation is a product of my judgement; it might be different, though not radically, in another's view.)

We may conclude this part of our analysis by observing that the substantive content of evaluation, covered in this section, relates to what issues are the most relevant to focus on and what kind of analysis is appropriate in each case. These two areas demand a high degree of technical competence on the part of the evaluation system.

TABLE 2

EVALUATION COMPLEXITY OF SELECT ENTERPRISES

Characteristic	UK		India		Kenya		Pakistan	
	British Steel Corp.	British Railways Board	State Electricity Boards	Modern Bakeries Ltd.	Industrial & Commercial Development Corporation	Mumias Sugar Co.	Pakistan Industrial Development Corporation	Karachi Electricity Supply Company
1. Organisational structure	A	A	A	A	A	C	A	C
2. Size	A	A	A	B	A	B	A	C
3. Product structure	C	A	B	C	A	C	A	C
4. Capital output/ labour ratio	A	A	A	C	A	C	A	A/B
5. R & D	A	A	B	C	A	C	A	C
6. Location	A	A	A	A	A	C	A	C
7. Monopoly	C	C	A	C	A	C	A–C	A
8. Market composition	C	C	C	C	B	C	B	C
9. Externalities	B	A	A	C	A	B	A	A
10. Financial viability	A	A	A–B	C	A	A	A	C
11. Special factors	C	C	C	C	C	C	B	C

3

The Systemic Requisites

It may be recalled that the underlying theme of this study is that, for the best results, evaluation has to be considered as a system, within which logical interrelationships should exist among the components. Two of these, viz., the purpose of evaluation and the content of evaluation, were discussed in sections 1 and 2. The present section deals with the requisites of evaluation, ranging over objectives, appropriate accounting, and performance indicators.

A. PRIOR DETERMINATION OF OBJECTIVES

This is the most important of the requisites and will, therefore, merit the most attention in this section.

The argument is familiar by now to students of public enterprise, that evaluation would be meaningful when the objectives of the enterprise are pre-determined (and agreed between the government and the enterprise);[26] or to put it in another way, that the objectives have to be determined in advance if evaluation is to proceed in a meaningful manner. The 1967 White Paper on Nationalised Industries, in the UK, evidences this argument: "Clear financial objectives ... serve as one of the standards by which success or failure over a period of years may be judged."[27] A similar idea is implicit in the suggestion, in 1976, by the National Economic Development Office (in the UK) that the annual report and accounts of a nationalised industry should contain a statement of its "financial and other criteria" and of "achievement against them."

To start with, let us concede this trend of thought and proceed to discuss the systemic requisites.

We have, for our first problem, five terms frequently encountered in the literature on public enterprise evaluation: obligations,

objectives, targets, performance aims, and performance indicators. The first two may be bracketed. The reason why the two are
distinctly mentioned is that in the UK, where a good deal of
thought has gone into this problem, "obligations" was the earliest
White Paper term.[28] This was later superseded, if one may say so,
by the term "objectives" (in the course of the 1967 White Paper).
In India the Bureau of Public Enterprise[29] and the Comptroller and
Auditor General[30] have been using the two terms together, "objectives and obligations."

Importance attaches to what the "objectives" connote. That
these are "wider" – to use the British White Paper description
(1961) – than in the case of private enterprises is clear. In fact that
is how the problem arises. For a useful set of objectives we have to
go beyond the general terms in which a case is made for public
enterprise: e.g., to fill gaps in private initiative, to help in the
development of underdeveloped regions, to assist in the government's distributional policies, and to be a model employer. The
search should be for objectives *specific* to an enterprise. They
cannot simply be financial objectives, except in the sense that these
may be set so as to deviate from the (ordinarily assumed) maximal
behaviour of enterprise managers (in the private sector). (Such a
step in itself implies the presumption of social objectives on
grounds of which a less-than-maximal financial objective is stipulated.) The non-financial objectives need determination, if
smoothness of evaluation in terms of set objectives is to be ensured.
For instance, a housing corporation may be given the objective of
helping low-income groups or industrial areas or specific classes of
people; an agricultural finance enterprise may be required to assist
small-scale farmers; an industrial finance enterprise may be asked
to focus on certain regions or on lending for further utilisation of
existing capacity rather than for establishing new capacity; and so
on. However, in practice, the functions or duties or objectives of
public enterprises are generally stated in too broad terms to be of
precise help in evaluation. For example, the British Telecommunications Act 1981 – one of the recent public enterprise Acts in
the UK – provides that:

Section 3

1. It shall be the duty of the Corporation (consistently with
any directions given to it under the following provisions of

this Part) so to exercise its powers as to provide throughout the British Islands (save in so far as they are provided by other persons or the provision thereof is, in its opinion, impracticable or not reasonably practicable) such telephone services as satisfy all reasonable demands for them.

2. It shall also be the duty of the Corporation, in exercising its powers, to have regard to –

(a) efficiency and economy;
(b) the social, industrial and commercial needs of the British Islands with respect to matters that are subserved by its powers;
(c) the desirability of improving and developing its operating systems; and
(d) developments in the fields of telecommunications and data processing.

3. Subsection (1) shall not be taken to preclude the interruption, suspension or restriction, in the case of emergency, of any telephone service provided by the Corporation.

It is difficult to see what specificity attaches to these provisions in such a way as to help in evaluation.

Just another instance of a "blank-cheque" criterion, from Kenya: The Industrial (and Commercial) Development Corporation is to have regard to the desirability of ensuring that any undertaking or enterprise (assisted by it) will be of long-term value in relation to the development of Kenya, whether or not it is likely to prove self-supporting or to furnish direct profits either immediately or in the future.

That the objectives as laid down in the Acts are too general is being realised by governments gradually. An apt illustration comes from the UK vis-a-vis the National Coal Board. As against the statutory generalisation (of 1946),[31] the Chancellor of the Exchequer tried to refine the objectives in terms of ensuring "a satisfactory return on capital while competing in the market place," to "aim at that share of the market which they can profitably sustain in competition with other fuels," and not to "plan on any continuing tranche of sales which will not be profitable."[32] These may not be precise enough; yet the direction of precision is clearly implicit.

Next, we come to the term "targets," with which "performance aims" may be bracketed. If objectives are supposed to have a relatively long-term angle, are "quasi-political" – to borrow a phrase from one of my discussions in the UK – and are clothed in indicative statements of preferences, targets are clearly quantifications applicable to a shorter term. These are not easy to determine, for they imply not only a correct choice of objectives in conceptual terms specific to an enterprise but also the quantifying of the results expected in a manner meaningful to the enterprise managers. Objectives of an undefined nature give rise to multiplicity of interpretations; and their value in evaluation may be meagre. Targets, on the other hand, are logistically more serviceable to evaluators. No wonder in the NCB case cited above, the Chancellor of the Exchequer added that the "satisfactory return" "will be quantified in due course."

Targets, like objectives, can be financial and social. That the former, i.e., financial targets, have to be specified in the case of individual public enterprises needs an explanation, considering that it is implicit in the concept of an enterprise that it works on maximising financial criteria. The need arises on the following grounds:

(a) Lack of clarity on the permissible effects of social obligations (assumed or stipulated) contributes to lack of direction in managerial motivation towards surplus generation.
(b) The absence of market discipline and fear of take-over or bankruptcy can dampen the level of managerial efficiency.
(c) A monopoly enterprise can raise exploitative levels of net revenues.

Financial targets can also have the good effect of forcing the government (and the enterprise) to be rigorous in the injection of social objectives in the operations.

In the UK, though considerations such as counter-inflation policy and social or sectoral objectives have been visualised, the financial targets have been considered as the "primary expression of the financial performance" (1978 White Paper, page 24); and attempts to evolve alternative indicators of efficiency have been few.

In view of the importance that attaches to targets as a systemic requisite under the argument we are considering, let us look deeper into this issue. The value of a financial target is qualified by at least four factors:

(a) *Surplus composition*

An overall surplus at the apex level of a large enterprise – and many public enterprises are large – is of limited value. Sub-targets have been fixed in a few cases in the UK – e.g., Intercity and Freight segments of British Railways Board; and Posts and National Giro-bank segments of the Post Office – but not in many others like the British Airports Authority, British Ports and Docks Board (Associated British Ports PLC), British Telecom and National Bus Company.

(b) *Price structure*

The precise cost basis of pricing is a point that merits enquiry in the context of an enterprise not exposed to competition. (It is on record that the marginal cost principle commended by the White Paper (1967) was found by NEDO (in 1976) not to have been adequately followed by several public enterprises.) Further, there is ample scope for cross-subsidisations by many public enterprises as organised today in most countries.[33] That the financial target is satisfied offers no necessary guarantee of efficiency without reference to these real determinants of the efficiency of operations. (It is of interest that National Bus Company (in the UK) realised the importance of "cross-subsidy from the relatively profitable to the unprofitable elements" of services and commissioned a study of the subject on its own initiative in 1982.[34])

(c) *Output*

The size of output is bound to be a major point of interest in several cases – e.g., railway train miles, Kwh of electricity and tons of fertiliser. A financial target might be met by the enterprise operating at different levels of output; and the enterprise operations might be neutral to the notion of the "socially" good option among them. British Railways Board is one of the few enterprises for which a physical output target is contemplated, though not quantified: "The British Railways Board shall from 1 January 1975 operate its railway passenger system so as to provide a public service which is comparable generally with that provided by the Board at present."[35] (It is not clear, from experience, that the government has developed a system whereby the output mix, apart from the total size, gets a public scrutiny.)

British Airports Authority is another example: it has a "performance aim" "to increase the number of passengers handled per employee by an average of 3 per cent per annum."[36] Probably this is more truly a productivity norm than an output norm; for its focus is eventually on keeping a rise in labour force below the rate of rise in output or keeping a fall in labour force above the rate of fall in output.

(d) Cost Level

In the case of a monopoly enterprise it would be necessary to be assured that the cost level represents a state of efficiency: or else reaching a financial target has little meaning. In the UK experience, there have been two methods in this respect. A cost reduction target has been set in some cases: e.g., a reduction in costs per passenger by 2½ per cent per annum – at constant prices – in the case of British Airports Authority, and reductions in "real-unit costs" (r.u.c.) by 5 per cent in non-gas activities of British Gas Corporation and British Telecom and by 1.5 per cent in National Bus Company.

The other device has been for the government to include in its references to the Monopolies and Mergers Commission cost review either in explicit or in implicit terms.

Even if we assume that these caveats are taken care of while determining the financial targets, what can be missing are the non-financial targets of the "social objectives" category. While perhaps not too severe in the context of the UK or of a developed country, this can be a material gap in a developing country where the social–returns potentiality of certain public enterprises is high indeed. Appropriately to individual enterprises some quantifications will be helpful, covering such areas as employment, investments in under-developed regions, technological development, product diversification, export stimulation, stimulus to ancillary or small-scale industries, and closures or expansions. The targets may be definitive – e.g., x or x per cent ...; they may represent the minimum – e.g., at least x; or they may be set in a range – e.g., between x and y. In their absence the managers do not know how far to go or where to stop. For instance, how far does an electricity enterprise go in rural electrification which does not pay well enough, how uneconomical can a plant be before it is closed, how adverse can the acceptable effects on productivity be of an excessive manpower that is not scaled down; how low can the acceptable export prices be in the interest of export promotion? And so on.

Analytically it is the social objectives that are central to the determination of objectives in the case of public enterprise. As an enterprise it need not be told explicitly that it should make a net revenue or that it should try to increase its level; it has only to be told when a contrary behaviour is preferred. Hence the need for financial objectives, translated into targets whose analytical justification depends, not so much on forcing the managers to raise a surplus as on the socially preferred deviation of enterprise behaviour from uninhibited maximality. Thus the notion of social objectives is implicit in the device of financial objectives or targets. The case for making the former explicit arises from the need to ensure that the managers of an enterprise are informed, in the full knowledge of the public, of what non-financial objectives are specifically assigned to them. Or else, one does not know what the social pay-off is (expected to be) for a given (less-than-maximal) financial target.

A few concluding comments on targets may be made at this point. First, what go popularly under the name of targets can be classified into different levels.

(a) The basic level: e.g., that the enterprise should earn a given percentage of return on capital employed, the terms being suitably defined.

(b) The qualifying level: e.g., guidelines or stipulations regarding pricing: "prices so as to reflect the costs at the margin of meeting demands on a continuous basis;"[37] targets of cost reduction, which are becoming progressively common in the UK; performance aims which have reference to the quality of output: e.g., "average level of train cancellations not to exceed 1.5 per cent,"[38] "90 per cent of first class mail to be delivered by the first day after collection."[39]

(c) The managerial level: e.g., performance aims on labour productivity: "to increase the number of terminal passengers per pay roll hour by ½% per annum . . . two fifths of the percentage

growth in terminal passengers over the three year period."[40]
(d) The means level: stipulations of the level of resources that will
    be available to the enterprise over a given period. Often termed
    a target, the External Financial Limits illustrate this category
    in so far as the UK nationalised industries – not all public
    enterprises – are concerned. A similar condition forms part of
    the "contrat de programme" in French parlance.

Second, the most essential focus of the targets should be on the
outcomes expected. They ought to be two-fold: financial and physical, to the extent it is deemed necessary to stipulate them under the
two distinctive heads. Implicitly they have to reflect the expected
social content in the operations of the enterprise. To restate the
point, if this were zero, the need for fixing targets would be
nominal, except to ensure that public enterprise managers are
minimally competent.

A word on cost targets. Analytically, they present an asymmetry
with revenue targets. In the latter case the object is to guide the
enterprise on the choice of a socially preferred surplus as against a
private enterprise surplus in like circumstances. As regards costs
the aim should be maximum minimisation possible; analytically, it
is doubtful if this needs setting, unless we buy the notion "without
it, managers do not think of it!" Any socially preferred deviations
from the least–cost approach are best spelt out as explicit constraints, accompanied by an adjustment in revenue targets or
appropriate compensations.

Finally there is an inherent problem in the whole area of objectives and targets (inclusive of performance aims). Do the latter
follow from the former, and do the several targets present mutual
consistency? Two simple examples suffice. A cost reduction target
set after a surplus target has been in force can only have the effect
of raising actual surplus beyond the target, other things being
equal; or perhaps, the other things may tend not to be equal and
the actual surplus may remain at the target level only – e.g., if
managers are lax in some non-cost directions. The other example is
a more familiar one – the adverse effects of EFL (a means target)
on cost reduction, on size and quality of output, on long term
growth and on surplus enhancement. Bits of evidence are available
on the British scene.[41]

Here is an interesting role that targets can play to remedy

internal inconsistencies among objectives, if laid down. Take the 1946 objectives statutorily set for the National Coal Board in the UK (cited in footnote already). They can be mutually incompatible with one another. One way in which to deal with the problem is to lay down targets under each objective such that within the quantitative structure of those targets conflicts of one being realised at the expense of another may not arise. This is not as easy as it sounds. Yet it can be a way out in a public sector situation where the so-called objectives are broad, if not wild – the more so in developing countries.

We shall refer to performance indicators briefly at this point. They do not have the significance of objectives or targets, though, when properly devised, they can reflect the way in which these have been achieved.[42] Experience suggests that they have come to possess a peculiar kind of relationship with targets. They seem to give ideas on what performance aims can be agreed as targets. In this sense some of the indicators have the value of being rolled back into targets; so it is useful for the managers, consumers and the government to evince interest in specifying and formulating them.

Reverting to our main argument, let us recall that our assumption so far has been that prior determination of objectives is necessary for evaluation. There are two problems about the assumption. First, it is, analytically, only partly true. Perhaps not too familiar or popular, this observation calls for an explanation. If we have the A–level evaluation in mind, prior determination of objectives or targets is not only helpful but necessary for the sake of adjudications on the content or merits of managerial performance.

When we proceed to the B–level of evaluation, prior determination of objectives and targets is essential in evaluating the rationale of governmental interventions, if any, in enterprise management and decision making. For instance, have the interventions been justified by, or adequate for, the objectives or targets? Apart from this, it provides us with an opportunity to evaluate the chosen directions in achieving a given social objective through a given public enterprise in comparison with other available modes of budget policy open to the government.

Here, more or less, the essentiality of prior determination ends. At the C–level of evaluation, where our concern is with how society views the actual results of an enterprise, and at the D–level where we seek to evaluate its overall comparative advantage, objectives as set are not our prime purpose; they do not hurt, though.

The other problem about the assumption of prior determination of objectives is that it turns out to be an unrealistic requirement in most countries. In fact, elaborate effort has been made in fixing objectives and targets mainly in the UK and in France. There is little in the rest of the world to approximate to it. (Some attempts have recently been initiated in Senegal on the French model of contracts.) It is probably fair to say that there have been no targets in India till recently, except for production targets in some cases and for recommendations on financial targets in a few cases like electricity and Port Trusts. If such happens to be the situation,[43] it stands to reason that we have to devise an evaluation system without the benefit of prior-determined objectives and targets. The evaluation has then to be conducted in the following stages:

(a) Could the managers, within any external constraints, have done better in commercial terms?
(b) What social returns accrued from their current structure of operations and what might they be if the managers moved towards better performance on commercial criteria?
(c) How incidental have any governmental interventions in operations been to whatever undeclared social objectives the government had in mind?

Even the first stage is good enough or timely enough in many countries. Over time such a direction of evaluation tends to induce the managers to focus on commercial behaviour; and governments will be compelled to formulate social objectives, if any, relevant to individual enterprises, which constitute a ground for their deviations from commercial behaviour.

There is a problem for the evaluator here. The situation is hardly so neatly one of total absence of objectives. The Acts contain some generalisations which lend themselves to diverse interpretations: e.g., "to satisfy all reasonable demands," and "to promote industrial development." Under these conditions it will be difficult for the evaluator to adjudge on how the enterprise measures up to any prior criteria and still less to blame the managers for any assumed shortfall.

The evaluator faces a problem of a different kind as well. Some managers begin to set for their enterprises elements of non-commercial objectives that they assume as appropriate – in the spirit of the Act or of the Minister's views in general. What sanctity they have, it is difficult for the evaluator to determine. Thus their relevance as a bench mark in evaluation is dubious, unless the government acquiesces in them in a clear manner.[44] (The point is not that the managers have no role in the evolution of the objectives; far from it; it is just that the objectives, to be operative as guidelines, should be agreed as between them and the government.)

Experience suggests that governments have, in general, not been effectively keen on setting objectives in clear terms, perhaps by design in many cases. It may suit them not to go beyond generalisations. It is in fact in the interest of managers that they should themselves ask for clear objectives or targets; where these are not forthcoming it will be good strategy on their part to propose performance aims or targets for governmental agreement. If they are in a position to insist on unqualified commercial behaviour in the absence of agreed objectives that qualify it, there is a good chance of agreed objectives evolving themselves. Or else, evaluation, in ultimate analysis, can never be an exact exercise; it cannot manifest itself as a system.

Before we turn to the next requisite of evaluation, let us refer to the "corporate plan" and the "contrat de programme." These could be a proxy for more open prior determination of objectives and targets and could materialise even if the latter were not available.

(a) The practice of *corporate planning* has been spreading among public enterprises all over the world. It serves, at the minimum, as a statement of the aims that the managers of an enterprise have set for themselves and therefore provides a bench mark against which their performance may be evaluated.[45]

Apart from this A–level function, the cross-section of corporate plans we come across present the following limitations as evaluation requisites.

First, the degree of commitment on the part of the government needed for a projected pattern of performance of the enterprise may not be there. The plan, at one extreme, may turn out to be a unilateral document. Whether the aims contained in it are realistic in terms of the likely resources, it is difficult to say.

Second, it is not certain that the corporate plan adequately incorporates the social or non-commercial objectives relevant to the enterprise – the more so when it lacks government commitment. Now the plan may serve the function of a managerial tool – good in itself, but not sufficient as a systemic requisite of evaluation.

Third, if objectives and targets go on emerging from the government from time to time, the purposefulness of the corporate plan as an evaluation requisite gets heavily qualified. However, as an internal document – binding the managerial behaviour at all levels – it has a place. The evaluator has to ask whether it is adequately rolled over with the knowledge of objectives and targets as they come and whether the internal logistics of managerial behaviour and control are suitably adjusted.[46]

(b) The *contrat de programme* – an essentially French method – represents a contract between the government and a public enterprise and covers many aspects of enterprise operations. Importantly it includes a commitment on the government's part as well, particularly in respect of the resources that will be made available and the managerial autonomy that will be permitted to the enterprise.[47] Other things being equal, such a contractual instrument smooths evaluation. Other things, in reality, are not always equal.[48]

B. APPROPRIATE ACCOUNTING

The second systemic requisite of evaluation relates to the quality of accounting. This can be reviewed in two aspects.

First, under conditions of inflation, accounting policies tend to be fluid even in advanced countries. Uniformity hardly exists in the valuation of current flows of revenue and expenditure and in that of assets and liabilities. Where revaluations are effected, an indeterminate degree of inconclusiveness characterises the different items found in the balance sheet. These problems are compounded when comparisons are attempted with previous years or other enterprises.

Secondly, we have the difficulties of accounting disaggregations under conditions of joint costs and joint revenues. Disaggregated revenue targets, and provisions against cross-subsidisations are no doubt important aspects of enterprise operations and must attract attention in exercises of evaluation. But the success of evaluation depends on the accuracy of accounting allocations within the enterprise.

This point is of interest with reference to many public enterprises like British Railways Board (which has sub-targets in respect of two of its several separable businesses), British Telecom (which has but one overall target, though its annual report disaggregates the finances right up to profit or loss among eleven categories of service), Indian Railways (which have widely divergent regional financial results), and Road Transport Corporations in India (where regional profitabilities are quite heterogeneous). It is of interest to note that the Monopolies and Mergers Commission (of the UK) commented on the Gas Corporation's accounts in respect of its appliances business; these deserved an appropriate monitoring so as to ensure that its accounting practices would not harbour monopoly practices inimical to the interests of competitors in the appliance trade.

Equally relevant is an excerpt from the MMC Report on the National Coal Board, concerning its accounting information which is found to be inadequate to "enable the management to base its decisions on an understanding of the cost of the capital that is likely to be involved, or the real profitability or otherwise of individual operations."[49]

There is then the question of the degree of competence available in the country in the computation of the costs attributable to the social objectives (or outputs) – for example, the "Social Railway," a term recently popularised in the UK. This is as important as the fact that a public enterprise has non-commercial objectives. This fact is of greater significance in developing countries; unfortunately the costing skills available to evaluation exercises are scarce.

C. PERFORMANCE INDICATORS

The third evaluation requisite relates to performance indicators. They are an aid to drawing inferences on how the results compare with those of a previous year or another enterprise, or with a bit of argument, on how they compare with what can be construed as possible. Their value in evaluation depends on the following questions:

(a) How good are they as averages?[50]
(b) Are they the right disaggregations relevant to the objectives, targets and performance aims envisaged for the enterprise?[51]
(c) How comparable are they over time or as between like enterprises?
(d) Do they together lend or add up to an impression that does not reflect the real status of overall performance in terms of financial and output results?

Public estimate of performance indicators found in progressive profusion in the annual reports of the UK nationalised industries is that they are inconclusive.[52]

Let us draw a conclusion at this stage. Evaluation is easier, at least at the A–level and partially at the B–level, if the systemic requisites such as objectives and targets are satisfied. In the real world these are hardly satisfied in adequate or meaningful measure. A blunt commercial evaluation may be possible but that is not what we want in the case of a public enterprise. Thus there exists an area of indeterminacy in the evaluation exercises. While the ideal is to remove it, the most practical aim should be to narrow it down consciously. Establishing the requisites helps in this process and serves the idea that evaluation intrinsically is a system.

In concluding this analysis let us briefly comment on the idea of an overall index of performance. Its origin, in a serious manner, may be traced to the "Productivité Globale des Facteurs" used by Electricité de France, to the point of incorporating it as a target, along with others, in the "contrat de programme" exercise. It is physical in nature, based on all factors used, unlike partial indicators such as labour productivity. However, its use has not been universal in the French public enterprise sector.

Qualifications to an overall index arise partly on statistical grounds and partly on substantive grounds. The former are the more familiar ones. For example, what aspects of the operations do we choose as the components? What is the degree of interrelatedness among them and when is an individual aspect to be considered as an independent component? What weights do we give to the different components? How correct is the scaling of the performance level, in respect of a component – e.g., into five ranges or four – and with what values for each range 1, 2, 3, 4, 5, or 5, 10, 20, 35, 40, or 5, 15, 30, 50, 75? Should these be the same for all enterprises?

The other set of qualifications is the more serious. We need to make an apparently semantic but fundamental distinction between performance measurement and efficiency evaluation. One can choose to assume that the two are the same; but the former, in terms of our analysis, corresponds to the A-level evaluation and can be of particular use in seeking a base with which to link the managers' eligibility to a bonus. (It is debatable, however, whether it is not preferable to link the bonus of specified categories of managers with accomplishments in their respective areas of operations and make overall profit or output the basis for bonus payments to those managers, particularly at the top, to whom that method is difficult to apply.) Evaluation, on the other hand, deals not so much with a *number* as with the *nature* of operations underlying it. For example, it is not just the net revenue percentage but the pricing practices underlying it, the cost conditions, the consumer satisfaction etc. that warrant evaluation. These cannot be fitted into the overall index.

Further, certain targets that go into the evaluation exercise, unlike in the global index, are not just statistical numbers of which some marked by under-accomplishment can be outweighed by others marked by over-accomplishment, but goals that have to be reached: e.g., reductions in work force, export earnings or investment in a backward region. One can argue that "weighting" takes care of this problem; it often cannot, satisfactorily. Hence a consolidated statistical number does little justice to the concept of evaluation where "social" or "extra-enterprise" goals are important; and most public enterprises have them.

We can deduce that an overall indicator has the danger of creating the impression that an x per cent improvement in it reflects improved efficiency. But it is just possible that the statistical result is at the expense of some almost compulsive goals. (No wonder the French Government insisted on complementing the Productivité Globale des Facteurs with return on investment and resources propres (cash flow) while finalising the "contrat de programme" with Electricité de France.)

Of course refinements can be suggested, to the effect that the overall index will be "evaluated" only subject to so-and-so minima being achieved in the accomplishments under goals A, B, C ...: a subtle retreat towards the quality-orientation of evaluation. Like targets in specific areas, the overall index can be an aid in evaluation; and in respect of certain physical results and bonus-determination it can be of particular value.

An overall indicator presents greater problems than an index in individual areas of operations or accomplishments, when we think of inter-firm or inter-temporal comparisons. Neither the components nor the weights are likely to be the same for several firms, even if in the same sector (or even for a given firm over a long period). To meet the disadvantage of the comparison ending up as an exercise in global numbers, one has to go back to the components (and several non-components) and their nature. The latter are what evaluation is expected to be keen about.

On balance, an overall or global index is of use in certain respects but is not an adequate substitute for the evaluation exercise.

4

The Agencies

We have so far dealt with three of the systemic aspects of evaluation: the level, the substance and the requisites. We shall now consider the last, viz., the agency.

In a limited sense the enterprise board itself has a role in evaluating performance at the different levels of management, vertical and horizontal, within the enterprise. This function assumes particular significance in the case of enterprises which are large in size, dispersed in location, diversified in market structure, and/or oriented towards the holding type of organisation. Many of the substantive items with which evaluation is concerned call for the board's attention in the first place; for in matters of disaggregation of targets, performance aims, results and accounting figures, the board has a basic role to play. No doubt external agencies draw their own evaluatory inferences and may have occasion to contest certain of the board's premises; but they cannot totally replace the board. The review of the UK experience in evaluation contained in the next section brings out certain specific institutional developments in progress within the enterprises themselves.

Let us turn to the more important, i.e., the external, agencies. Broadly they are of two kinds: governmental and non-governmental. The former may be subdivided into executive or departmental agencies and others.

Departmental activities – i.e., activities of the sponsoring ministry, the Treasury and any other departments of government – strictly come under the caption of monitoring and control, and border, even if implicitly, on participation in the processes of decision making, and in the continuing exercise of making sure that the managers are on the right track in the eye of the government. There is an interesting paradox here. The more the departments exercise these functions, the more they are "participating" in enterprise decision making, perhaps in management and in the direction of the results. And the case for B–level evaluation is building up. Thus the department's role is "controlling" and "facilitating" rather than evaluation, except for any functions of evaluation assumed by them either under a specific government decision or in the absence of any well-designed process of outside evaluation. The Indian account in the next section will illustrate this point with reference to the Bureau of Public Enterprises in the Ministry of Finance; so does the Nepal section with reference to the Corporation Co-ordination Division of the Ministry of Finance.

The non-departmental agencies enjoying the stamp of government are principally two: the Comptroller and Auditor General (CAG) and Parliamentary Committees. Our comments on them will be brief and analytical.

The CAG has access to all records and probably reasonable knowledge of what records and information exist on any issue under query. And he has a high degree of independence. As against these two unique advantages, expertise is not his trump card, though he can call for expert assistance. (The Indian account in the next section illustrates this possibility.) Another problem stems from the controversial virtue of the CAG entering the arena of value judgements to which the evaluation processes are bound to lead him at some stage. In any case neither is it his function, nor has he the expertise, to go into the propriety of any objective or target set; his interest is more in the effectiveness of a managerial process – a good aim in itself but not sufficient in a system of evaluation.

A typical comment on the nature of the CAG's reviews of public enterprises comes from the Multisectoral Commission of State Enterprises of Peru:[53]

> The Comptroller General's control system, essentially legalistic in nature and based on the examination of the firms' procedures, was accused by the Commission as "asphyxiating, immobilizing and crushing state owned enterprises." Controls were applied with such a counter-productive excess of zeal as to be characterised as "abuse of authority, absolutist and omnimodal power (causing a rupture of management and institutional authority)."

Empirically speaking, the CAG is empowered with the audit of public enterprises in several countries. In some cases he is the exclusive auditor; in others he has the option; in a few he does not enter the picture at all, e.g., in the UK. The trend in the developing world is towards the extension of his coverage, in the name of efficiency or propriety audit. The main object and justification lies in the realm of parliamentary control of public sector finances rather than evaluation in a systematic manner. No doubt it can be one of the bits that add up to whatever evaluation exists.

Parliamentary Committees – Estimates and Public Accounts Committees originally, Select Committees on Public Enterprises lately in some countries (in the UK, India, Sri Lanka, Bangladesh etc.) and Departmental Committees in the UK today – are unique in many respects. They are independent of the executive wing, can call even ministers for evidence and delve into probable interventions (or interferences) by the government in (or with) public enterprise decisions and operations (as recently evidenced in the case of the non-closure of the uneconomical Ravenscraig integrated steel plant of British Steel Corporation) and take initiative in the emergence of socially oriented value judgements. The major drawback is lack of expertise, despite the privilege of seeking it on an ad hoc basis. Further, evaluation of public enterprises is too intensive and demanding a task for Parliamentary Committees to cope with. Undoubtedly the Committees have a valid role in the system of evaluation, especially at the B–II and C–levels. In some countries like Sri Lanka there is an attempt to widen their remit so as to "monitor efficient performance."[54]

Among the most purposeful in a good evaluation system today are the non-governmental agencies such as Price Commissions, Pay Boards, and Monopoly Commissions. They are bi-sectoral in coverage and deal with specific substantive aspects of operations whether in the public or in the private sector. Though they are not designed – still less set up – to undertake evaluation, certain elements of evaluation are implicitly covered by their methodology and enquiries. In fact the terms of reference to the MMC in the UK do often contain such phrases as the following: "To report whether the National Coal Board could ... improve its efficiency;"[55] and "the scope for improvements in efficiency and manpower productivity."[56]

I have included in my study on decentralisation of control in public enterprise the relative merits of independent commissions. They apply in substantial measure in the context of evaluation. Their superiority over departmental agencies of evaluation may be expressed in the following terms. Departmental evaluations are fundamentally under the impact of the government's or the minister's political interests; they tend to be over-defensive of the performance, partly for reasons of departmental involvement in enterprise decision making and management. Besides, in countries where changes in government are infrequent, departmental evaluations can turn out to be docile and far from being rigorous.

A word on my proposal for the establishment of a Public Enterprise Commission. The case for it, detailed in Part III of my book *The Nature of Public Enterprise*, is all the stronger when we talk of evaluation. It can be sufficiently expert and independent. It can devote itself consistently and exclusively to public enterprises – the whole range of them. It can be a focal point for co-ordination of any bits and pieces of investigatory and evaluatory findings emerging here and there all the time. It is particularly purposeful in respect of levels B, C and D. As regards highly specialist analyses it can invite assistance from outside, even as the MMC does. Above all, it can be an excellent sister institution to Parliamentary Committees in providing the public with overall conclusions on the net purport of individual or all public enterprises to the nation.

The extended use of the MMC in the UK today for "efficiency audits" of public enterprises illustrates, in de facto terms, a partial version of the PEC idea. The functions of the recently created CONADE in Peru[57] and, more obviously, of SIGEP in Argentina,[58] amply validate the rationale of a PEC type agency. Countries which lack agencies such as the British MMC with effective coverage of public enterprises – and there are many such – will surely benefit from the establishment of a PEC type agency. A recent example of a country where professional thinking is building in favour of a PEC is Nepal.[59]

Such an agency can minimise the need for the constitution of enquiry commissions in respect of given enterprises. The latter can be limited to exceptional cases.

The systemic inter-relationships between level and substance on the one side and agency on the other may be illustrated in a tabular presentation (Table 3). Column (2) indicating the most preferred agency and column (3) suggesting the next best, represent my views. The reasons for the preference may be inferred from the preceding pages. The last two columns serve the purpose of showing how the "actual" position in the UK and India compares with the "preferable" position. Entries in columns (4) and (5) are approximate and should not be taken as too exact.

It may be recalled that the systemic inter-relationships as between level of evaluation (i.e., A/B/C/D) and agency have already been indicated in Section 1.

Another tabulation (Table 4) is presented below just to indicate the great diversity among countries in the institutional basis available for evaluation in the context of public enterprises. Certain gaps are conspicuous – e.g., the monopoly commission has no remit on public enterprises in India; parliamentary committees do not exist in Malaysia; the CAG has little role in the UK, and there are no consumer councils almost anywhere except in the UK. What all this implies is either that a certain needed input of expertise is not at work or that it is supplied by a second or third best agency. In either case reforms will be necessary.

Let us draw conclusions from this part of our analysis.

First, most of the items meriting evaluation seem to be appropriate for an independent PEC type of agency. (The MMC of the UK resembles it in some respects.)

Second, evaluation is different from monitoring and control. The ministries are fitted for the latter but very nominally for the former function. Even the monitoring is not effectively done by them in several countries. This, in fact, justifies non-departmental evaluation of their role in public enterprise performance – analogous to the B–level of evaluation.

Third, at some points of C–level analysis and partly of B and D–levels what can come out of an evaluation agency is an expertly processed presentation of "leading" optional scenarios and not definitive "yes/no" conclusions, for the authority for the latter may alone come from Parliament in several cases. The evaluating agency cannot be considered to be the judge on the propriety of the social results of an enterprise's operations. Given the guidelines, it can draw reliable inferences.

Fourth, the evaluation agency has to be provided with balanced expertise, power of access to data, guidelines on non-commercial or social preferences, and reasonable protection against reprisals.

Last, there will be great value in obligating the top board of an enterprise, especially of a large enterprise, to present a periodic statement (in some form) of the processes and conclusions of its internal evaluations. These substantially help external evaluations.

TABLE 3

SYSTEMIC AGENCY RELATIONSHIPS WITH EVALUATION ISSUES

Item (1)	Most preferable agency (2)	Next best agency (3)	As of now UK (4)	As of now India (5)
1. Organisational structure				
a. Holding complex				
(i) Overcentralisation	Public Enterprise Commission (PEC)	Consultants	–	
(ii) & (iii) Cross-subsidisations	PEC/Monopoly Commission	–	Mono. Com.	
b. Integration				
(i) Transfer pricing	PEC/Monopoly Commission	–	Mono. Com.	
(ii) Pricing	Monopoly Commission/ Price Commission	–	Price Com./ Mono. Com.	BICP[1]
(iii) Economies	PEC/Monopoly Commission	–	–	
c. Ownership status				
(i) Management capability	PEC	Consultants	Mon. Com.	BPE[2]
(ii) Anti-social results	PEC	–	–	
2. Size				
a. Largeness	PEC/Monopoly Commission	Consultants	–	Ministries
b. Excess capacity	PEC/Monopoly Commission	Consultants	Mono. Com.	Ministries
c. Internal reorganisations	Consultants	Mono. Com.	–	
d. Cross-subsidisation	Monopoly Commission/PEC	–	Mono. Com.	
e. Too small	PEC/Consultant	–	–	

(continued)

		Mono. Com.	Ministries
3. Product Mix			
a. Utilisation	Consultants	–	
b. Cross-subsidisation	Monopoly Commission/PEC	–	
c. Disaggregated financial targets	PEC/Government		
4. Capital–output/labour ratio			
(i) Degree of utilisation	Consultants	–	
(ii) Margin of substitutability	Consultants	–	
5. R and D	Consultants		
6. Location			
(i) Diseconomies	Board/Consultants	–	
(ii) Social subsidisation	PEC	–	
(iii) Production decisions	Consultants/Monopoly Commission	Mono. Com.	
(iv) Industrial relations	PEC	–	

1. Bureau of Industrial Costs and Prices.   2. Bureau of Public Enterprises.

(Table 3 Continued)

Item (1)	Most preferable agency (2)	Next best agency (3)	As of now	
			UK (4)	India (5)
7. Monopoly				
(i) Effects	Monopoly Commission	–	Mono. Com. Parliamentary Committees	
(ii) Social preferences	PEC	–		
(iii) Inefficiency	Monopoly Commission	PEC	Mono. Com.	
(iv) Public Interest	Monopoly Commission/Government	PEC	Mono. Com.	
8. Externalities				
(i) The Results	PEC	Ad hoc Committee	CPU[1]	
(ii) Financial implications	PEC	Ad hoc Committee	Parliamentary Committees	CPU
(iii) Consumer impacts	PEC	Ad hoc Committee	CPU	CPU
(iv) Managerial inefficiency	PEC/Consultants/Monopoly Commission	–		
9. Financial viability	PEC	Consultants	–	
10. Special factors	PEC	Ad hoc Committee	–	

1. Committee on Public Undertakings.

TABLE 4

EVALUATION AGENCIES IN SELECT COUNTRIES

Agency (1)	UK (2)	India (3)	Pakistan (4)	Kenya (5)	Malaysia (6)
Board	√[1]				
Holding Company	–	☆	√	☆	☆
Consumer Council	√	–	–	–	–
Commercial auditors	√	☆	√	☆	☆
Government auditors	–	√	√	☆	☆
Ministries					
Sponsoring	√	☆	√	☆	√
Treasury	√	√	☆	√	☆
Cabinet secretariat	√[2]	–	–	√	√
Special arrangement					
– Interministerial	–	–	–	☆	–
– Expert cell	–	★	√	–	–
Mono. Commission	√	–	–	–	–
Price Commission	√[3]	√			
Pay Board/Wage Board	√[3]	√			
Special PE Commission[4]	–	–	–	–	–
Parliamentary Committees	√	√	–	√	–
Special Committees	√	☆	–	–	–
Management Consultants	√	☆	–	☆	–

Notes

1. E.g., Audit board; Efficiency wing.
2. E.g., Central Policy Review Staff; National Economic Development Office.
3. Abolished recently.
4. E.g., SIGEP (Argentina), CONADE (Peru).

☆ represents some semblance of the notation.

★ Ad hoc – such as Expert Committee on Public Sector Undertakings (1980–83) and Pathak Committee on Public Sector Undertakings (early 1970s).

5

Empirical Reviews

This section is devoted to a review of the evaluation experience in certain countries chosen from different regions. The aim is to highlight the salient features of the experience and comment on them from the analytical angle of this study. No attempt is made to provide a comprehensive historical survey of the problem in these countries.

A. THE UNITED KINGDOM

The UK, with its long experience in public enterprise, presents several points of interest in the context of evaluation.

(a) *The requisites*

The Acts governing the nationalised industries contained provisions that had a flavour of social obligations: e.g., "to collaborate in the carrying out of any measures for the economic development and social improvement of the North of Scotland District or any part thereof" (Section 2 of the Hydro-Electric Development (Scotland) Act of 1943); "To secure, as far as practicable, the development, extension to rural areas and cheapening of supplies of electricity." (Section 1(b) of the Electricity Act of 1947)

And the financial provision that accompanied such generalised objectives ran on the following lines: "to secure that the revenues ... are not less than sufficient to meet the outgoings ... properly chargeable to revenue account, taking one year with another." (Section 13 of The Electricity Act, 1957)

Such provisions allowed the managers' decisions to "touch on social policy upon which Parliament should pronounce," and allowed them "to realise an indeterminate surplus."[60] I observed in 1959, with reference to British electricity, that it was desirable "to institute certain rules in order to encourage objective performance" by the enterprises.

It was not until the 1961 White Paper came that systematic thought was given to the "issue of their wider" obligations. It was after the next White Paper on nationalised industries in 1967 that financial targets (also termed "objectives") were fixed for individual nationalised industries. Evaluation, in a sense, would then be easy, if it meant the comparison of actual net revenues with the targets.

There were two serious qualifications. One was that most of the systemic requisites of evaluation (outlined in Section 3) were too inadequately and ineffectively provided for. Second, though "parenthetical" mention was noticeable, the real content of social objectives has not been specified, by and large.

In effect what existed have been financial targets, but not objectives. Analytically targets should flow from objectives but here the reverse process has been at work, in two ways.

Over the last few years there has been an effort to formulate performance aims. For instance, accompanying a financial target, two performance aims – "to reduce costs ... per terminal passenger by ½% per annum" and "to increase the number of terminal passengers per pay roll hour by ½% per annum" – were fixed in 1983 for the British Airports Authority. In some cases, e.g., the Electricity Council, discussions have been in progress between the government and the Electricity Council "with the object of establishing a number of performance aims."[61]

While such measures [62] provided some necessary accompanying conditions for financial targets, put pressure on cost reduction under conditions of monopoly and helped move the targets in the direction of objectives, the other method of refining the objectives in themselves has also been in progress. The statement of the Chancellor of the Exchequer relating to the Central Electricity Generating Board (CEGB) and the National Coal Board, in March 1983, illustrates the point.[63] Though the prime objective set for CEGB is "maximum efficiency," attaining "the lowest possible cost" – an aim intrinsic to any enterprise, certain specific shades of objective have also been provided; and this is an improvement, methodologically: for example, "to explore and exploit the full potential of nuclear power to contribute to the cheap, effective and safe production of electricity," and to "set prices so as to reflect the costs at the margin of meeting demands on a continuing basis."

Likewise, in the case of the NCB, mention may be made of the objective "to earn a satisfactory return on capital while competing in the market place," and "to aim at that share of the market which they can profitably sustain in competition with other fuels ... not plan on any continuing tranche of sales which will not be profitable."

Great importance has been attached, besides, to the formulation and presentation, in annual reports, of performance indicators, ever since the 1978 White Paper. British Railways Board outlines 21 of these in its annual report for 1982 – for the years 1978 to 1982, besides providing four indicators comparing British Rail with averages of eight European railways. The Post Office cites, graphically for 1977–83, 16 performance indicators in its annual report for 1982–83. And so on. These help evaluation in terms of how much "this" year's performance, bit by bit, compares with a "past" year's or with another enterprise's. But they do not reflect conclusive substance on evaluation in its comprehensive sense.

One of the proxy requisites of evaluation has been the corporate plan. It would amount to a full-fledged basis for evaluation at certain levels if it were understood to be a bi-laterally committed document – approximately like the French "contrat de programme" – in which are incorporated all major targets (and performance aims) reflecting the objectives. But the actual situation in the UK nationalised industries, as a cross-section, is still far from such an ideal position.

There is one other instrument wielded in the UK most effectively, namely, the "external financing limit" (EFL). This represents the ceiling of outside borrowing by the enterprise. It has strictly a "means"-of-operations connotation; yet it has been termed frequently as one of the targets. For example, it is shown under "a number of targets and objectives" in the Post Office annual report for 1982–83 (p. 6). It is listed as the first among "financial objectives" in the British Railways Board's annual report for 1982. The annual report of British Gas Corporation for 1982–83 states: "there are three formal targets established between British Gas and the Government for the monitoring of the Corporation's financial performance – a financial target, an external financing target and a performance target." The weight attached to the EFL has been such that the CAG was hard put to observe that, where it conflicted with the financial targets, "it was not clear ... which took precedence."[64]

This much for the objectives, targets and indicators, on all of which there is much to be desired in the UK, in spite of the continuous attempts towards improvement. One broad conclusion may be drawn. There has been no effective search for determining the social or non-commercial objectives, on the whole, except for any that have been implicit in the performance aims, if any were agreed.

At this point let us turn to a brief comment in terms of the level–approach to evaluation. The UK experience is almost wholly of the A–level, focused substantially on the performance of the managers. Evaluation at the B–level is not consciously undertaken and has trickled down in tiny bits when the MMC made guarded factual references to "external" impacts, and Parliamentary Committees made obvious comments on the ministerial influences. But as to whether the interventions have themselves been good for the national economy on intrinsic grounds – and not on corporation–autonomy grounds – there has been too little of helpful evaluation.

As for the C–level, little seems to be consciously envisaged; for the "social" instrumentality of the nationalised industries has not been defined adequately. Whether privatisation, just initiated, will leave only the relatively non-commercial segments of activities in the nationalised sector and will therefore make imperative the C–level evaluation in the future, it is difficult as yet to speculate.

The D–level has not been undertaken, either, though a great deal of privatisation has been unleashed in several sectors of nationalised industry. In the absence of specific evaluations of comparative advantage, privatisation measures might appear to some as ideological.

(b) *The agencies*

Let us turn next to the agencies which have remit in public enterprise evaluation in the UK.

In the early years after nationalisations too little thought was given to evaluation. Herbert Morrison observed, in 1953: "on the whole, I want the Board to take care of themselves."[65] He even preferred the method of a periodical inquiry to a Parliamentary Committee "once in a matter of about seven years"[66] on the lines of the BBC inquiry that had taken place in 1949.[67] The Parliamentary Select Committee on Nationalised Industries was probably the first "external" agency entrusted exclusively with functions that covered several aspects of evaluation of these industries.[68] In spite of reservations in certain quarters, the Select Committee proved to be highly useful (i) in bringing to public and Parliamentary notice information relevant to evaluation, (ii) in expressing views on matters closely linked to the evaluation of the enterprises, (iii) in bringing to light ministerial interventions and their impacts, and (iv) in providing a friendly and understanding forum for the enterprises themselves. In terms of our analysis the Select Committee served a purpose at the B–level and to a limited extent at the C–level.

Changes were effected in the system of Parliamentary Committees in 1979, resulting in the abolition of an exclusive Select Committee on Nationalised Industries. Instead, these enterprises would come under the jurisdiction of the appropriate Departmental Committees. The Industry and Trade Committee, the Transport Committee and the Energy Committee have the bulk of the nationalised industries under them. The Departmental Committees look at a whole industry; and "there is no one body with power to oversee general matters which relate to all the nationalised industries."[69] Though there was a provision for establishing a sub-committee drawn from some of the relevant committees, from time to time, to consider any matter affecting two or more nationalised industries, this never materialised. Cross-sectional evaluations therefore have become less frequent today, though some of the Departmental Committees – e.g., the Treasury and Civil Service Committee, the Industry and Trade Committee, and the Transport Committee, did produce reports of broad interest to all nationalised industries, especially in their financial aspects.

The next external agency we should refer to is the National Board for Prices and Incomes (NBPI). Though not set up for public enterprises or for evaluation, this body has covered partial evaluations of enterprise efficiency, along with suggestions on its improvement. Though it had to work within "the background of the government's policies for the nationalised industries, including the financial target for the relevant period,"[70] it did make useful observations of the B–level type.

Then came the Prices Commission, which, like NBPI, was neither exclusive to public enterprises nor concerned with evaluation, but bore a somewhat similar relationship to both, in respect of the enterprises referred to it.

The Monopolies and Mergers Commission has since 1981 become the most significant independent agency concerned with the efficiency of nationalised industries. The Government has already referred to it a large number of nationalised industries and plans to refer each industry to it about once in four years. The membership of the MMC has been suitably strengthened. The MMC, it is claimed, "will remain the main instrument for the external scrutiny of these industries."[71]

The terms have generally contained such phrases as the following: "without reducing the standard of service provided, improve its efficiency"[72] and "the extent to which any deficiency in the quality of service provided is the result of inefficiency; the scope for improvement in efficiency."[73]

The Reports produced by the MMC bear the stamp of expertise,[74] on the whole, and correspond to most part of the A–level of evaluation, and a few aspects of the B and C levels. It has the following limitations, however:

(i)   It has no volition of its own. It can only take up an enquiry on reference from the minister.

(ii) Its evaluations are limited by the terms of reference set by the minister. These can be too restrictive in some cases.

(iii) It does not have the same access to records as the CAG has, nor can it call for evidence from the minister as the Parliamentary Committees can.

It is not impossible to remedy the last handicap if Parliament so chooses. Experience suggests that probably the MMC's reports have not seriously suffered from lack of information or of powers to seek information.

The government, further, intends to commission independent consultants to carry out "efficiency audit" – e.g., of the British Gas Corporation.[75] The Serpell Committee on British Railway Finances, appointed by the Secretary of State for Transport, was in response to the Board's suggestion for "an independent examination of the railways' current financial position and its probable financial requirements over the next decade."[76] It may probably be placed within the category of independent consultants rather than of a once-in-seven-years overall evaluation conceived by Herbert Morrison.

At this stage mention may be made of consumer councils, an essentially British institution in the public enterprise sector. Even if in a limited area, they can play a role in providing a profile of how consumers value the services rendered by a nationalised industry. The councils have a particular role to play in the case of monopoly organisations, to which category most of the UK nationalised industries belong in substantial part. Their real value in a system of comprehensive evaluation lies in providing useful information on how the consumer, for whom the output is intended, feels about it.

Two governmental agencies which have played a part in public enterprise evaluation, not on a continuing basis but in an ad hoc manner, are the National Economic Development Office (NEDO) (in 1975) and the Central Policy Review Staff (in 1981–82). (The former is a tri-partite body and the latter, in the Prime Minister's Office, was disbanded in 1983.) Neither is intended as a specific means of evaluating individual enterprises; but both have reviewed cross-sectional issues in some depth in the recent years. The studies by NEDO aimed at "a wide-ranging enquiry into the role of the nationalised industries in the economy and the way in which they are to be controlled in the future."[77] The 1978 White Paper followed this study.

The CPRS was invited by the government, in 1981, to consider the relationships between the government and the nationalised industries and the monitoring of the financial performance of the industries. One of its recommendations was that "clear objectives" should be quantified. The government decided in 1982 "to agree strategic objectives with each industry consistent with its statutory duties, financial targets and performance aims."[78]

(c) *Conclusions*

Let us draw a few conclusions from the UK experience.

First, there has been no attempt to set up an exclusive evaluation agency for the nationalised industries; even the Parliamentary Select Committee has ceased to exist. An exclusive Efficiency Audit Commission ("to assess the work of the nationalised industries")[79] in any version of William Robson's proposal, has not been favoured.

Second, it appears that, on the whole, greater stress has been laid on which agency might be entrusted with some version of the task of evaluation than on what it was that was sought to be evaluated. The latter, to the extent seriously considered, appeared to be encapsulated, even as recently as in 1981 at the hands of the CPRS, into "the (poor) financial performance of many of the industries." The issue of social functions and their synthesis with the financial objectives has not been consciously tackled in earnest or with success.

To dilate on this observation a little further: as the policy of privatisation materialises, evaluations of the C and D levels become necessary, in order to provide a non-ideological justification. There is no serious attempt to do this yet. Further, the activities that will remain in the public sector, even after some privatisations take place, will clearly call for the B and C levels of evaluation in order to assure the public that their operations and their financial implications are exactly what society wants, assuming that we have some knowledge of this.

Third, there are several "mixed" enterprises in the UK. With privatisations, their number is likely to grow, covering such significantly publicly owned enterprises as the Associated British Ports PLC (with 48½% shareholding by the government). The most effective of the evaluation techniques, including the MMC references, do not seem to cover these. They will be limited to the so-called nationalised industries. Of course it is possible that, though the "mixed" enterprises do not fall within the purview of Section 11 of the 1980 Competition Act, they may, on other criteria, be considered as fit candidates to be referred by the minister to the MMC.

Fourth, the CAG has had no role in public enterprise audit/ evaluation in the UK. A possibility long dormant, his role came up for active discussion in the recent days and there was in fact a private member's bill seeking to give the CAG "inspection rights to carry out economy, efficiency and effectiveness examinations of the use of resources by nationalised industries, publicly owned corporations and any company of which more than 50 per cent of the voting shares are publicly owned."[80] Eventually the National Audit Act 1983 did not include these bodies within the CAG's

preview. However, there has been a new development worth com-
mending. The government has welcomed reports by the CAG on
the effectiveness of the monitoring done by the sponsor departments. These can contribute substantially to the B–level evaluations, considering, in particular, the CAG's unique position. But
the reports, on his own admission, do not "set out to examine the
efficiency of the industries themselves."[81]

Finally, there is an interesting development within some of the
nationalised industries: to set up an Audit Committee, consisting
of some directors. British Steel Corporation was the first to do so.
Originally it was to look at financial as well as efficiency aspects,
covering among others financial indicators. These latter aspects
were, however, abandoned gradually. Its main usefulness lies in
ensuring that the external auditors receive the necessary assistance
from the executives of the Corporation and in reviewing the work
of the internal audit department. Though not an "external"
agency of control, the Audit Committee, if properly composed,
could greatly help the top board in conducting whatever role it was
designed to have in self-evaluation. (The three members of the
Audit Committee were drawn (during 1982–3) from the non-
executive section of the board.)[82]

Another intra-enterprise development worth recording is the
establishment of an "efficiency studies" wing – e.g., in the
National Coal Board. This wing reports once a quarter to the Audit
Committee consisting of three non-executive board members.
This, at the minimum, is a measure of self-criticism.

One last comment. The many qualifications and questions
raised in this section on the UK experience do not negate the fact
that it is one of the few countries in the world that have given
serious attention to evaluation and that have really achieved some-
thing tangible. The point simply is that it does not represent
systemic perfection.

B. ARGENTINA

The unique feature of Argentina in the context of evaluation
relates to the working of an exclusive institution called Sindicatura
General de Empresas Publicas (SIGEP). This was set up about the
same time as the Corporacion Nacional de Empresas Publicas
(CEN) was wound up, with functions that significantly included

the exercise of external control over public enterprises and evaluation. As per recent changes in law, almost all public enterprises in the country come under its jurisdiction; those relating to the Armed Forces are the only exception.

SIGEP is better equipped to cope with performance evaluation than the former CEN. In substantive terms it is conducted at three inter-linked levels, denominated at x2, x1 and x0. x2 represents the macro-economic level and SIGEP's reviews under this head tend to bring out the national factors of relevance to an enterprise under evaluation. These may range over the balance of payments position, the government budgetary situation, the level of economic activity and trends in growth of GDP, general financial conditions including rates of interest, and the inflationary conditions. x1 relates to the sectoral level and seeks to codify the circumstances of direct relevance to the enterprise within the sector concerned. x2 and x1 are in the nature of a backdrop against which evaluation of an individual enterprise can be socially meaningful, the more so if national policies are concretised and targets set – which, unfortunately, is not the case in Argentina. x0 concerns the enterprise level. Any findings at x0 level can be understood in the broader context of x1 and x2 factors. For example, improved traffic revenues of the railway system – a part of the x0-level findings – can be evaluated in terms of the management's efficiency or any windfall (extreme) circumstances like bumper harvests, discovered from the x1 and x2 reviews.

At the x0 level, the most vital part of the evaluation, SIGEP produces nine chapters, which together seek to present a comprehensive technical, economic and financial profile of the enterprise. These relate to: (1) planning, control and information systems, (2) marketing, (3) operations (production), (4) economic situation, (5) financial situation, (6) investment plans, (7) human resources, (8) quality of service, and (9) goal fulfillment. Chapter (1) has particular importance in that, in the absence of externally indicated targets or objectives, the existence or otherwise of internally set parameters is a matter of interest in the context of evaluation.

Besides the annual volumes containing the nine chapters, SIGEP produces quarterly reports, monthly reports and special studies. These have a clear role in the public information system that is of relevance to the effectiveness of evaluation.

On the basis of the factual situation presented above, let us draw conclusions of interest in our analysis of evaluation. First the positive points:

(a) SIGEP covers almost all public enterprises. Its functioning can represent, and be aimed as a conscious response to the evolution of, a system of evaluation relevant to enterprises in the public sector, as against the emergence of bits of review and investigation.

(b) SIGEP possesses many organisational advantages. It is located within the Presidency of the Republic through the Planning Secretariat; it is well staffed; it is composed of three ex-officio official members and three others to be appointed by the President – one of the latter will be the President of SIGEP; it seems to have been accepted as a useful tool by government agencies as well as public enterprises; and its staff has continuing relationships with the enterprises, including participation in Board meetings.

(c) The x2, x1, x0, technique is intrinsically a useful element in evaluation. That it is adopted, as a system, is commendable.

And now a few qualifications:

(a) The x2, x1, x0 technique first. Excellent in principle, this raises two problems. First, apart from providing some description of the macro and sectoral situations, it does not reflect any conclusive set of objectives or targets relevant to a given enterprise; nor does it enlighten anyone on the issue of synthesising among disparate ends or considerations. Second, it leaves open the real problem of evaluating the social results of an enterprise, though it certainly helps by providing a data base. Experience may show how to deal with this inadequacy on its part.

(b) Evaluation is one of SIGEP's functions. Control is another; and it can end up as the more important one in practice. It is even possible that the more effective its control function the less impartial its evaluation exercise. (Paradoxically, through its control functions it acquires a participatory role in the enterprise performance!) Time will show if the soundness of its evaluations is outweighed by its control concerns. Its internal organisation is, in fact, heavily geared to the mechanics of control. The three substantive divisions are: General Syndic

(Legality), General Syndic (Auditing), and General Syndic (Performance Control). Evaluation seems to be intertwined with control in the last division.

(c) There is, finally, a basic problem common to all evaluation systems in economies such as the Argentinian, where inflation is so galloping as to make reliance on financial indices highly questionable. Emphasis, then, shifts to physical parameters; and quantitative conclusions on efficiency become less easy, partly because of non-homogeneity of the diverse indices – e.g., tons produced, numbers employed, and inventories. SIGEP, however, is in a position of advantage in that it can formulate devices of comparison on a system-wide basis, and can also evolve the necessary procedures of inflation accounting that minimise the degree of non-comparability among magnitudes that refer to diverse inputs or outputs, enterprises, and points of time.

C. MALAYSIA

The major interest of this example stems from the fact that Malaysia is one of the few countries that have a Ministry of Public Enterprises. One may expect, prima facie, that it represents the institutional response on the government's part to the need for a centralised or co-ordinated focus on public enterprise matters and that one of its good effects can be the evolution of a "system" of evaluation.

The Ministry (MPE) was set up in 1974. It does not have all public enterprises under its jurisdiction. Essentially concerned with the State Economic Development Corporations, three financial institutions (Development Bank, Malaysian Industrial Development Finance Ltd., and Komplex Kewangan Malaysia Bld.), Urban Development Authority, Agricultural Development Corporation of some States, and road transport licensing, its focus has been on those activities that have material reference to the strengthening of Malay or "Bumiputera" participation in the economy (and in property ownership). Even in this respect it has recently suffered a bit, in that the major complex of Majlis Amanah Rakyat (MARA) moved to a new Ministry of National and Rural Development. Several other ministries have public enterprises under them; and the huge Pernas, a holding complex with hundreds of subsidiaries in the field of industry, is under the Prime Minister.

The MPE's status is not in fact that of an all-public enterprise ministry. For this reason it does not have the authority to evolve and implement a system of evaluation applicable to all public enterprises on a comprehensive basis. Nevertheless, some of the most persistent efforts at establishing an evaluation mechanism have been made by it. A UN project on performance evaluation gave fillip to the efforts during 1979–83. (There has been a similar project in the Ministry of Land and Regional Development as well.)

The Implementation and Co-ordination Unit (ICU) located in the Prime Minister's Department, has a data base, which includes public, along with other, enterprises. ICU is strategically located; it constitutes the Secretariat to the National Action Council whose Chairman is the Prime Minister, and offers advice to the Council. For instance, several public enterprises were closed down on its recommendation in 1981. There is some semblance of the D–level of evaluation here. ICU's evaluations are, by and large, financial in nature. The major social criterion it upholds is Bumiputerisation which happens to be a basic tenet of the National Economic Policy (NEP).

A development that can be of value consists of ICU providing the authority for a co-ordinated system of evaluation on an all-public enterprise basis, with MPE offering specialist technical inputs, designed primarily on the basis of the enterprises within its own jurisdiction. The fact that MPE's own rationale stems from the NEP, which is one clear motive, or result expected, of the Malaysian public enterprises, is an advantage in the course of such a development.

Two comments seem relevant. Whatever evaluation exists is done under government auspices and is open to limitations that the A–D level analysis of section one suggests. Besides, there is no appraisal of social efficiency except in terms, at best, of Malaysiation (or Bumiputerisation).

On the whole, it appears that the following conclusions of a Malaysian scholar on evaluation hold good:[83]

(1) There are a number of evaluation and decision centres with no formal and explicit locus of performance evaluation

co-ordination; (2) the evaluation and decision centres generally do not have explicit statements of purpose, which thus
contribute to the low performance; (3) the system is very
closely linked to the planning and implementation systems to
the extent of becoming diffused with them; (4) the system
lacks adequate resources in terms of quality and quantity; (5)
the performance evaluation approach developing independently in different evaluation centres is characterized by the
absence of specific, clearly stated and formal criteria and
indicators of performance, biased towards micro level performance and dictated by perceived problems, and lacking in
time program basis; and (6) the characteristics of the administrative dimensions affect evaluation operations to the extent that these operations are generally not conducted objec-
tively and systematically.

D. NEPAL

This section brings out, among other things, the implications of a
"small" economy for evaluation. Nepal has a large number of
public enterprises spread over all sectors. Probably most of the
modern industrial activities of a medium or large size are in the
public sector. The total capital employed amounted to Rs. 3.5
billion in 1980–81. This presented a 60% increase over the 1976–
77 figure and would reflect a basic dimension of the national
economy, viz., the imperativeness of public enterprise.

A major factor that has attracted the government's interest in
evaluation is the continuously poor financial performance of most
public enterprises. In the aggregate, gross profit (before interest
on loans) declined from 3.6% to 3.1% of capital employed between
1976–77 and 1980–81. And the figure of total cumulative losses
rose from 10% of capital employed in 1976–77 to 17% in 1980–81.

Before we review the arrangements currently contemplated, let
us look at the unique substantive features of the evaluation exercise.

First, there are Nepal's fundamental handicaps in development.
Most enterprises are – and are bound to remain – small and infra-
optimal. In order for them to operate in the best possible manner,
attention has to be focused on the economics of size, so as to ensure

that wasteful multiplicity is minimised in a given sector and that, more importantly, export competitiveness is developed. It is relevant in this connection to search for international joint ventures that may help reduce the diseconomies of local smallness and facilitate the availability of wider markets.

Equally basic is the topographic and demographic factor. Most part of the population is sparsely spread over difficult terrain, so much so that the costs of supplying them with electricity, food, fertiliser etc. are bound to remain relatively high – almost permanently. Nepal Electricity Corporation (NEC) illustrates the point. The average intake of power per consumer tends to be low as it seeks to reach consumers beyond the present 4% of the population; the transmission inputs tend to be high; and the degree of utilization of supply networks in individual regions tends to be uneconomical.

A meaningful conclusion follows. Evaluation becomes an aspect of national development strategy. Attention needs to be given to the question of how far certain elements of high cost are intrinsic to the economy, rather than being directly characteristic of the operations of given public enterprises. Expert quantifications would be needed in order that the right results of evaluation ensue in fairness to the enterprise.

This is a special version, in Nepal, of the C–level evaluation. To turn to the NEC example again, the immediately prospective expansions in the supply network will be followed by a behaviour of costs that is unlikely to approximate to the law of decreasing costs, for reasons of topography and demography. There may well be a hump in the cost curve. How soon it slopes down, we cannot assert as of now. If the investment programmes are determined on technical and intrinsic grounds of long-term economy, evaluation of current performance (for a pretty long period) has to allow for the argument suggested here. The question, in one form, will be: how much of NEC's cost is to be accorded the status of a social cost? This has far-reaching implications. At the minimum it can help control cross-subsidisations among NEC customers.

This issue has relevance to Royal Nepal Airlines Corporation as well. Discussions indicated that the cost curve of domestic services would in fact rise as output expands in the near future.

Second, the need for evaluation at the B–level, i.e., of the enterprise as a whole, is particularly great in the Nepalese context.

For, the governmental involvement in direction and management of public enterprise is extremely high – even of the structured variety (i.e. the B I level). The Auditor General's comment is on record that "undue interference comes from the Ministries concerned, but policy direction is never given."[84] A detailed analysis of data (for 1978–79) shows that 60% of all directors of public enterprises were civil servants; and another 18% came from public enterprises. The material point here is not whether other sources are dependably large, but that evaluation has to keep an open eye on the sure impacts of an "external" origin on enterprise performance. These are heavy for another reason: nearly half the total number of chief executives are civil servants on short-term secondment. Add to this the fact that there is an almost total absence of functional directors. Even the chief executive (or general manager) was not on the board except in some 13 out of 52 enterprises in 1978–79. One other fact: quick turnover of the chief executive has been quite common. We can identify 22 cases of general managers who served in that capacity for a year or less, and 19 who served between one and two years, as per the data gathered by the Corporation Co-ordination Division.

Third, the need for subsidies is rather wide spread in the public enterprise sector of Nepal. Specific provisions are prior-determined in the case of Nepal Food Corporation, Agricultural Input Corporation, and Jute Development Trading Company. Whom precisely do these subsidies benefit? Should the rice or fertiliser subsidies be available to hills and to Kathmandu in equal measure? Is there not a real subsidy to National Electricity Corporation today, which added a loss of Rs 32 million to the accumulated figure of Rs 1.31 million in 1981–82, *without* taking into account the cost of equity capital (of Rs 400 million)?[85] To what extent is the subsidy involved in these finances to be evaluated as a national development cost and who precisely benefits from it? Questions such as this will long remain an important remit of evaluation in Nepal.

Further, there has been an unfortunate trend in the overall financial results, as the following diagram shows.

The total capital employed has been rising over the recent years (1977–81), but gross profit rate and the value added per unit of capital have been falling. The "capital lost" figure has been rising. One of the first tasks of evaluation would be to look into the merits

FIGURE 2

SOME FINANCIAL INDICES OF PUBLIC ENTERPRISES IN NEPAL

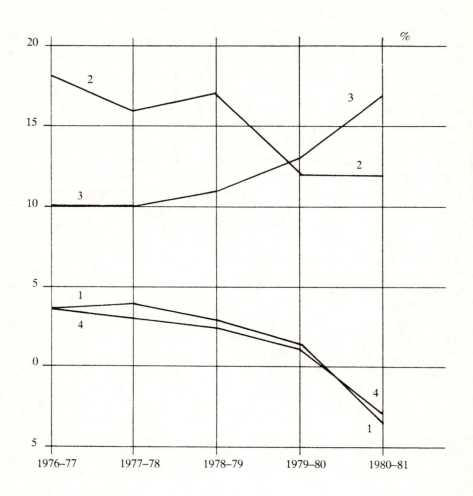

1. Gross profit as per cent of capital employed
2. Value added per unit of Rs. 100 of capital (in Rs.)
3. Accumulated loss as per cent of capital employed
4. Gross profit per net sales of Rs. 100 (in Rs.)

of these trends in a dis-aggregated manner, i.e., enterprise-wise and sector-wise, and examine the social trade-offs, if any, in individual cases. Is the situation, in certain cases, one of no perceptible social returns despite financial losses?

Some of these questions border on the C–level of evaluation concerning the social results. There is, finally, the D–level, relating to comparative advantage, whose relevance to Nepal is enhanced by the recent policy promulgation by the government, of encouraging private investment, privatisation of certain public enterprises, and cautious new investment in public enterprises.[86] How realistic the implementation will turn out to be, it is difficult to say, considering the rather limited investment initiative in the private sector. Yet the point should not be missed that evaluation has to probe issues of comparative advantage so that the right decisions on entrepreneurial change may be canvassed. In fact the term comparative advantage has to be given a really comprehensive meaning, so as to cover such ideas as the social costs of letting private monopolies into small market sectors and of creating a situation in which privatisations enjoy success but at the expense of benefits to "remote", "rural" or handicapped areas of the country.

We shall now turn to about the only machinery for evaluation contemplated in Nepal – viz., the Corporation Co-ordination Division (CCD) of the Ministry of Finance. It is interesting to note that the government intends to provide for the major systemic requisite of objectives and targets. CCD is expected to "redefine" the objectives of individual enterprises, in consultation with the supervising ministries and the enterprises concerned, and ensure their quantifiability as far as possible. Also annual targets regarding capacity utilisation, output and profit are intended to be fixed for each unit appropriately with its nature and objectives.

A word on "indicators" at this stage. From CCD's *Performance Review of Public Enterprises in Nepal (Macro and Micro Studies)* issued in 1981, there is a disproportionate emphasis on financial ratios – standardised for all the 52 enterprises covered. That these, by themselves, have limited meaning cannot be over-emphasised. Tailor-made indicators, physical or eventually garbed in financial terms, are necessary for individual sectors, if not enterprises.

The data are tabulated under "economic and financial indicators" – too ambitious a title for what is found underneath it.

"Value added" is perhaps the one indicator outside of usual financial ratios. But then a caveat is worth bearing in mind. Is an absolute increase in it invariably a good index? Assume that a revenue addition is just offset by a wage addition. Apart from the wage results, what net benefit has the enterprise conferred on society? (Is the wage result itself to be considered a social benefit in the circumstances of the national economy?) Besides, how does the value added figure appear in relation to the capital employed? Aggregate figures under this head, cited in the graph in this section, raise serious doubts on this as an "absolute" index.

It is as regards the substance of evaluation that CCD merits appreciation. Having selected a sample of 21 enterprises for the first shot, it has identified some specific substantive issues demanding evaluative attention in the context of individual enterprises. Considering the freshness of the approach, we may find it useful to excerpt the scope of their survey in broad outline as follows (Table 5 below). (Compare this with section 2 on typology.)

To this typology list may be added issues concerning the basic developmental context of the national economy and the evolving trends of comparative advantage in respect of individual public enterprises, as discussed earlier in this section. Further, there are

TABLE 5
TYPOLOGICAL APPROACH TO EVALUATION

Characteristic (1)	Enterprise (2)
1. Managerial processes	
a. How have the PEs utilised their resources?	1. National Commercial Bank
	2. National Insurance Corp.
b. What efforts have been made for management development? (Corporate plan, MIS, service quality)	3. Agricultural Development Bank
	4. Nepal Industrial Development Corporation
2. Sickness	
a. Inter-ministerial effort	1. National Trading Ltd.
	2. Raghupati Jute Mills
b. Direct monitoring by the Finance Ministry	3. Nepal Transport Corporation

3. Pricing Policy

a. Monopoly or competitive pricing	1. Royal Nepal Airlines
b. Measures of cost control	2. Tele-Communication Corp.
c. Cross-subsidisations	3. Nepal Electricity Corp.
	4. Nepal Oil Corporation
	5. Timber Corporation
	6. Dairy Development Corp.

4. Subsidy circumstances

a. Cost control measures	1. Nepal Food Corp.
b. Distribution system	2. Agriculture Inputs Corporation

5. Capital re-structuring

	1. Royal Nepal Airlines
	2. Raghupati Jute Mills

6. Procurement and foreign exchange

a. Procurement price control measures	1. Nepal Oil Corp.
b. Foreign exchange budgeting	2. Agriculture Inputs Corporation

7. Managerial autonomy:

a. Areas for further autonomy	1. Janakpur Cigarette Factory
b. How to control PEs as autonomy extends	2. Birgunj Sugar Factory
c. How have profits been earned?	3. Himal Cement Company

8. Mergers and privatisation

a. Organisational reform	1. Timber Corporation
b. Possibility for divestiture	2. Fuel Corporation
	3. Raghupati Jute Mills

9. Determination of performance criteria

a. Short term/long term	All sampled PEs
b. Physical/financial/social	

10. Top management audit

a. Performance of Board of Directors	By sample
b. Performance of Chief Executive	
c. Performance of Operating Supervisors	
d. Performance of Middle Management	

enterprises other than those selected under the sample under a given characteristic, which also deserve evaluative focus – e.g., Royal Nepal Airlines Corporation and Nepal Electricity Corporation under "subsidy;" and Royal Nepal Airlines Corporation under "foreign exchange."

We now turn to the final aspect of the review, viz., the agency. Two comments are possible.

First, there seems to be room for ensuring that the boards of directors themselves conduct adequate and effective monitoring and evaluation of managerial processes, behaviour and performance, so that their evaluation constitutes a useful basis for external evaluation. Not enough is yet done on their part in Nepal. In fact CCD is anxious to influence the boards in the direction.

Second, CCD, in spite of its vigorous programme on right lines, has the limitation of being a government agency – in respect of the B, C and D levels of evaluation. If it is not immediately easy or realistic to expect expert "outside" skills, the case for CCD as an evaluation agency currently tends to be strong. But the time should come, sooner rather than later, when the full range of evaluation as a systemic whole should be appropriately accomplished through the establishment of an independent commission on the lines elsewhere discussed in the present study. The CCD can then continue to function as a data base, as a monitoring cell, and as an admirable link between public enterprise on the one side and governmental agencies on the other.

CCD was set up in 1980 as a successor to the former Corporation Co-ordination Council (which was located in the Cabinet Secretariat). It is under a Special Officer of Secretary's rank (who has several other portfolios in the Finance Ministry). The Chief Economic Adviser of the Ministry operates as Adviser to CCD also. There are two Under-Secretaries – one for Fiscal Management and the other for Policy, Planning and Evaluation. Each of them has two junior officers under him. The staff is small in size – an inevitable constraint on its extent or depth of functioning. Even the 21 enterprises selected as a sample for specific evaluation reviews will be covered, hopefully, in a period of two years as per present plan. It is easy enough to infer from its staff structure that its maximum utility rests on concerning itself with strategic aspects of monitoring, as against the assumption of the total exercise of evaluation.

E. PAKISTAN

There are four aspects of the evaluation processes in Pakistan that deserve prefatory mention.

(a) Almost all public enterprises are organised within holding corporation complexes: e.g.,

> Federal Chemical and Ceramics Corporation Ltd., with 12 subsidiary or operating companies under it (in 1982);
> State Engineering Corporation Ltd., with 10 subsidiaries;
> Pakistan Automobile Corporation Ltd., with 11 subsidiaries; and
> State Cement Corporation of Pakistan with eight subsidiaries.

> This arrangement resulted from a measure of reorganisation introduced in 1973, consequent on wholesale nationalisations that touched almost the entire sector of organised industry.

(b) The Ministry of Production, set up in 1972, represents a ministry of industrial and commercial enterprises in the public sector – some 63 units in 1983. It does not cover all public enterprises, though. The nationalised banks, other financial institutions, transport and communications units, the gigantic Water and Power Development Authority and other electricity enterprises, the departmentally organised railways etc. are outside its jurisdiction. The ministry has a highly diversified, but not exclusive, charge of the public enterprises of Pakistan.

(c) An Experts Advisory Cell was set up in 1980 as a professional body attached to the Ministry of Production. By virtue of the expertise that it enjoys, as contrasted with the Ministry, it has laid claims to tasks of evaluation.

(d) The Comptroller and Auditor General has recently entered the scene of evaluation with a specialist performance evaluation unit under his jurisdiction.

The Experts Advisory Cell (EAC)

This is a unique institution, in several ways, in public enterprise parlance. It was set up as a fairly independent agency attached to the Ministry of Production and composed of professionals –

accountants, economists and engineers. It has a Board of Governors consisting of the Minister of Production as Chairman, the Secretary and the Additional Secretary of the Ministry, and two corporation chairmen (by rotation). The Chief of EAC acts as the Board's secretary.

The functions of EAC are as follows:[87]

  (i)   Formulation of proposals for financial restructuring and re-organisation of the Companies and Units.
  (ii)   Review of the annual budgets in respect of production, sale and profit of the companies and units.
  (iii) Overseeing and evaluating the performance of each holding Corporation, Company and Unit.
  (iv)   Preparation of monthly, quarterly and annual performance reports.
  (v)   Special management and proprietory audit of Corporations, Companies and Units as and when required.
  (vi)   Determination and coordination of annual plan targets for production and investment and ensuring that these targets are achieved.
  (vii) Processing of schemes for balancing, modernisation and expansion of existing Units and Companies and setting up of new projects.
  (viii) The monitoring of the implementation of ongoing projects. Identification of bottlenecks in the completion of projects on time and within the sanctioned costs.
  (ix)   Collection and collation of data of the operating companies and new projects for other Federal Ministries and Organisations.

Broadly, as mentioned in the Resolution establishing it, EAC is devised as an assistance to the Ministry of Production "in the performance of its functions."

EAC's work ranges over three stages: information system, performance evaluation system and incentive system.[88] The evaluation processes adopted by EAC are interesting and represent a well-directed attempt to deal with the intrinsic complexities of the problem.

As a first step, it lays down the performance criteria it deems relevant to specific individual enterprises. (By implication, these are not uniform in every case.) As a second step, it assigns weights to the criteria, admittedly "at the risk of some subjectivity," the more so in the case of non-commercial objectives. (The weights are agreed with the enterprise concerned.) The third stage consists of compiling a composite performance indicator. The fourth stage relates to the fixation of a target for the following year and the ordering of varying degrees of improvement over target under each criterion over a scale abbreviated into five grades, 1 (the highest) to 5 (the lowest). At the next and final stage, in so far as evaluation is concerned, a weighted grade of achievement is computed for each enterprise.

Here is an example (Table 6). The criteria in column (1) are not exhaustive; and they can be different among different enterprises. The weights, in column (2), can also vary from enterprise to enterprise, as against individual criteria. (For instance, training may be of very high importance in one enterprise and R&D of little moment, whereas in another, the reverse may be the case. Likewise, export earnings may be of significance in a given case, while it may not be relevant to another at all.) The scale of percentage improvements (in achievement) over targets may be quite different from criterion to criterion and from enterprise to enterprise. It depends on what appears to be – and then is agreed as – reasonable in the precise context of a given enterprise at a given unit of time. It is in this way, that due allowance can be made for the diverse structures of constraints, technical, marketing or financial, that different enterprises work under.

Two further aspects of the exercise merit notice. One is, strictly, incidental to evaluation, however important it may be to the fortunate managers in material terms. Depending on the grade achieved, they will be entitled to performance bonuses on the following scale:

Grade A   3 months' additional salary
Grade B   2 months' additional salary
Grade C   1 month's additional salary
Grade D   15 days' additional salary
Grade E   Nil

The other aspect is of intrinsic substantive interest. It relates to the concept of public profitability. This is computed as follows:

PUBLIC PROFIT

=   Private profits (after tax)
+ Direct taxes
+ Interest payments
− Financial incomes
+ Depreciation
− Opportunity cost of working capital
− Subsidies
± Adjustments

Yet another highly important step is under contemplation, viz., making "social adjustments" in respect of non-commercial objectives. The expenditures concerned will be considered, not as a cost, but as a dividend-in-kind contributed by the enterprise to the government.

TABLE 6

PERFORMANCE EVALUATION SYSTEM

A. AGREED WEIGHTS AND TARGETS

Criterion	Weight	% Improvement Targets				
		High 1	2	3	4	5
(1)	(2)	(3)	(4)	(5)	(6)	(7)
Public Profitability	50%	25	20	15	10	
Private Profitability	20%	40	35	30	25	20
Corporate Planning	10%					
Training	10%					
R & D	5%					
Indigenisation	5%					

B. RESULTS ACHIEVED

Criterion	Weight	Achievement	Item Score	
			Raw	Weighted
(1)	(2)	(3)	(4)	(5)
Public Profitability	.5	20%	2	1
Private Profitability	.2	25%	4	.8
Corporate Planning	.1	Very Good	2	.2
Training	.1	Good	3	.3
R & D	.05	Excellent	1	.05
Indigenisation	.05	Poor	5	.25

So much for EAC's evaluation function. EAC also implements monitoring of the performance of enterprises. On the plus side the claim is made that, unlike the ex-post-facto evaluation, this permits "intervention" during the year. Naturally it has founded an elaborate data base and reporting mechanism, and publishes monthly and quarterly performance reports, annual review and annual report. Due stress has been laid on developing a uniform cost accounting system – a major systemic requisite in terms of our analysis. EAC submits periodic cost reports on the enterprises for the use of the Ministry of Production and the corporations in monitoring operations.

The Comptroller and Auditor General (CAG)

Decision was taken in 1977 "to establish on a permanent basis a special unit to evaluate on a continuing basis the performance of public sector commercial enterprises."[89] The unit consists of specialists in accounting, management etc. It does not have any authority over the enterprises, nor can it interfere with management discretion. (In some ways here lie subtle differences from EAC.)

This unit does not have "responsibility for routine audit" – a difference, in principle, from the Indian situation in comparable cases. Its main responsibility will be "full assessment and analysis, according to sound commercial and business standards of performance and efficiency, of the operating results of the enterprises."

This unit is assigned the duty of keeping up-to-date accounts of government investments and returns.

"To ensure the independence of the unit" it is constituted as a part of the Auditor-General's set-up and its reports will go to the Public Accounts Committee, besides the Ministry of Finance.

The CAG unit started working early in 1979, with a Director General and, under him, six teams of two officers each, of whom at least one is a qualified accountant. Each team spends six weeks with an enterprise and after discussions with the management, produces analyses and conclusions on finances, sales, profitability, purchasing, production, marketing, personnel, organisation, management system and future prospects.

Not every enterprise is covered every year. The focus is on helpful appraisal rather than on fault-finding.

O&M Division

The O & M Division of the Government touches the area of evaluation tangentially, in that, either at the request of individual enterprises or at the instance of the cabinet, it looks into the affairs of enterprises from the O & M angle and provides agreed reports capable of implementation. The headquarters of Water and Power Development Authority, Karachi, and Electricity Supply Corporation are among those examined by the Division so far. The work accomplished by the Division cannot be characterised as evaluation; it represents, rather, a consultancy service. Many small and medium-sized enterprises may not be able to undertake the work from out of internal staff resources. Even in other cases the O & M Division comes in handy to the government in ensuring that an organisational review that is deemed necessary because of public complaints or any other reason does in fact take place at a competent and dispassionate level.

Comments

There is little doubt that the efforts being made in Pakistan in the field of evaluation represent a clear and well-deliberated advance over the earlier situation in that country and over the kind of arrangements that prevail in many other parts of the world. However, the following comments merit notice.

First, as regards EAC:

(a) The processes of evaluation as yet undertaken by EAC represent an effort at reviewing the managers' performance, analogous to the A–level of evaluation in terms of our analysis. This is confirmed by the way in which a year's financial magnitudes are all recompiled, after allowing for price changes, so as to make them comparable with a past year's figures. In other words, how well have the managers performed "this" year as compared with "last" year (or, a point for later examination, as compared with "set" targets)? This, certainly necessary, work is what can – and strictly, ought to – be done by the sectoral holding companies themselves, which, as we have seen, are a distinctive and deliberately designed aspect of the public enterprise system in Pakistan. They do not seem to be adequately used for the purpose of management reviews and inter-firm evaluations within given sectors. This function, instead, is lifted to the EAC level, with two possible consequences, viz., that its sectoral experience is likely to be inferior to that of the sectoral corporations and that it is likely to set the holding corporations against EAC at several stages in the battle of wits on criteria, weights, targets and grades.

(b) As for targets etc., apart from the complexities inherent in any such negotiations, there are two fundamental gaps in the EAC system. The first is institutional: it is doubtful what "public" sanction exists for the "agreed" targets, criteria, weights and grades negotiated by EAC with the enterprises. True, the point has not yet attracted notice from the executive and other wings of government. But it surely will, the more so when bonus eligibilities begin to be established and at some stage arrest the Treasury's attention. The degree of commitment on the part of the Ministry of Production and the Ministry of Finance in the main and of the other agencies like the Ministry of Planning and the Cabinet agencies as well, is unclear, considering EAC's constitutional status and its jurisdictional limitations to about 50 per cent of the public enterprise sector.

The second is a substantive gap. Little is done (yet) on the identification of the "public" or extra-enterprise aspects of the public enterprises evaluated by EAC, followed by all the subsequent steps in their appropriate treatment. The example of an "uneconomical" location – the one that is often cited during discussions – is but one instance. There exist many more subtle cases of internalisation of externalities; and some of these basically reflect the nature of involvement of governmental agencies themselves. It is for this reason that the analytically distinctive stages of B, C and D have been emphasised in our discussion. EAC's remit, as practised today, falls short of these disiderata. As the externality aspects of public enterprises get drawn into the evaluation system, the institutional inadequacy of EAC will stand out clearly. (It is relevant to note that the "operating and financial indicators/ratios" uniformly compiled for all the public enterprises under its purview – see Appendix 1 – border on internal financial management only.)

(c) EAC's enthusiasm to compute public profitability through adjustments to the figure of private profitability derived "raw" from the accounts is commendable. Yet it is worth noting that the method can apply equally to private enterprises too (though the latter have no interest in the computation) and that the most material ingredients in the computation in the case of a public enterprise, viz., the non-commercial obligations of (or impacts on) it, are yet not adequately, if at all, considered.

A simple retort is possible, viz. that "social adjustments" are only a question of time; (and that they are provided for in the system as devised through World Bank assistance). Here is a problem, though, that will call for discrete attention. It is easier to identify and compute the financial effects of forces that infringe on managers without their choice than to establish which of these, or to what degree any of these, are admissible as indicators of public profitability. Not all of the former are. It is at this stage that an intricate interface between the government on one side and the enterprises on the other will develop. This cannot be helped; only it has to be anticipated and duly provided for. EAC may not find itself best placed to steer this issue.

(d) Two other issues of logic may be presented at this stage. First, how successfully does an evaluation process so blatantly linked to managerial bonus payments establish itself as an intrinsically sound system of evaluation in the first place? Do problems connected with bonus payments weaken the focus of evaluation itself and develop indifference on the part of one or both of the negotiating sides on criteria, targets, weights, and grades? Second, can one institution – EAC – combine in itself the two functions of monitoring and evaluation? The former is an essentially ministerial function and it is good that it remains so – as in fact is the case with the public enterprises outside the jurisdiction of the Ministry of Production. Can an agency performing a ministerial function be effective as an evaluating agency?

Perhaps in the nature of advance doubts, these questions have fundamental validity as time will show.

To conclude: it is not clear how far EAC enjoys the commitment of the government; nor is it sufficiently of an external agency for full-fledged evaluation. A specific issue, not faced yet, is the attitude of the Ministry of Finance to EAC's grading-cum-bonus methods and to its "social adjustments" computations, when made.

A good point that cannot be missed is its emphasis on target-setting as a tool of evaluation. This has systemic cogency, as may be seen from section 3 of this study, though Pakistan, through EAC, has a long way to go in evolving a total system of evaluation ranging over A–to–D levels.

As regards the CAG unit:

(a) The methodology adopted by the unit is essentially one of financial analysis. (At several points, it overlaps EAC's work, except for the interest of the latter in adjustments for arriving at public profitability.) It does not appear to cover the idea of propriety, usually claimed on behalf of the CAG elsewhere – e.g., in India. Perhaps it is not wrong to say that its techniques and findings can equally well apply to a private enterprise. And what may, at best, be accomplished is an appraisal of the manager's financial performance. The unit's concept is one of systematic periodic examination of an enterprise to identify its strengths and weaknesses and arrive at meaningful recommendations for improvement in key operational areas.

(b) Unlike EAC, this unit does not proceed in terms of set criteria or targets. Its approach is one of historical comparisons.

(c) Like EAC, it does not delve into questions of governmental impacts on enterprise management.

(d) The CAG's unit enjoys credibility and attracts the attention of the Public Accounts Committee.

Two final observations. First, the absence of machinery for evaluation of the entire public enterprise sector is a serious gap. Second, there is special need for the D–level evaluations bringing out the precise degree of comparative advantage enjoyed by individual public enterprises, especially because of the newly evolving national policy in favour of privatisation in some sense of the term. The policy will stand on firm ground if such evaluations precede decisions on entrepreneurial changes.

F. INDIA

What is attempted here is but a brief appraisal of the problem of public enterprise and evaluation in India. It is so proportioned, in length and angle, as to constitute an integral part of the total study. At several points, therefore, one needs to look back to the analytical passages of the first four sections for the underlying arguments.

A. *Nature and extent of public enterprise*

It will be helpful to start with a grasp of the magnitude of the problem as reflected in the nature and extent of public enterprise in India.

At the outset, the share of public investment in total investments during the 1980–85 plan period is 53 per cent. In so far as transport, electricity, manufacturing, finance and trade are concerned, the proportion is much larger.

(a) Investments in central government enterprises totalled Rs 247,61 crores by 1982, spread over 203 enterprises.[90] These are exclusive of investments in departmental enterprises such as railways, posts and telegraphs, and broadcasting. There are several other public enterprises not covered by the BPE figures; the major ones being the nationalised banks and major port trusts.

Then we have large numbers of public enterprises – about 600 – at the state government level, on which neither analytical nor evaluative focus has been adequate so far. It is difficult to adduce reliable figures. One instance, viz., Andhra Pradesh (A.P.), may be cited, just to suggest that these investments have a considerable magnitude. The total government investment in 65 operating enterprises was Rs 962 crores (by 1982) in A.P. The total for all states, on this illustrative basis, would compare fairly with the central figures.

(b) The sectoral spread of the investments is wide enough to cover the entire range of economic activities: infrastructural, manufacturing (heavy and consumer goods), services, and finance. The broad composition of the BPE segment is shown in Table 7.

(c) The enterprises are of quite diverse sizes. Many of them are very large and occupy the top places on the national scale. Some of these are statutorily monolithic – e.g., Bharat Heavy Electricals Ltd., Hindustan Machine Tools Ltd., Indian Drugs and Pharmaceuticals Ltd., and Heavy Engineering Corporation Ltd. (The first three are multi-locational; and all are multi-product.) Some

TABLE 7

SECTORAL SPREAD OF PUBLIC ENTERPRISE (1981–82)

Sector 1	No. of enterprises 2	Investment (Rs crores) 3
Enterprises producing and selling goods		
Steel	6	49,08
Minerals and Metals	13	23,43
Coal	5	27,25
Petroleum	12	20,70
Chemicals, fertilisers and pharmaceuticals	21	35,73
Heavy engineering	14	12,27
Medium and Light engineering	19	4,11
Transportation equipment	11	7,48
Consumer goods	12	5,06
Agro-based	10	24
Textiles	12	5,50
Enterprises rendering services		
Trading	18	7,58
Transportation	9	17,06
Contract and Construction	7	1,88
Industrial development and technical consultancy	9	1,01
Development of small industries	1	38
Tourist	2	49
Financial	3	1,301
Section 25 companies	3	61
Insurance	7	67
	203	247,61

Source: BPE, op.cit., p. 138.

others are "holding" complexes – e.g., Steel Authority of India Ltd., Coal India Ltd., and National Textiles Corporation Ltd.

The classification of public enterprise sizes shown in Table 8 illustrates the diversity.

(d) The investment process has been significantly continuous since 1961:[91]

TABLE 8
PUBLIC ENTERPRISE SIZES (BY CAPITAL EMPLOYED)
(1981–83)

Capital employed (Rs crores) (1)	No. of enterprises (2)
Below 10	66
10–25	36
25–50	14
50–100	18
100–150	12
150–200	6
200–500	17
500 and above	10
	179

Source: BPE, op.cit., pp. 31–41.

At the commencement of the third plan
  (1961)   Rs   9,53 crores
At the end of the third plan (1966)   24,15
At the commencement of the fourth plan (1969) 39,02
At the commencement of the fifth plan   62,37
At the end of the fifth plan (1979)   156,02
At the commencement of the sixth plan (1980) 182,25
As on 31 March 1982   247,61

(e) The public enterprise sector includes several joint ventures: among public agencies themselves, and between public and private investors. Foreign capital obtains in some cases. The joint ventures with private investors are more prominent at the state than at the central level.[92] For instance, 99 per cent of equity in BPE enterprises is from the central government; and the foreign share, essentially in loan capital, is 10 per cent (1982).[93] As for state government enterprises, the A.P. picture is as follows: 53 per cent of the total investment is from the state government, 11 per cent from the centre, five per cent from financial institutions, and 30 per cent from "outsiders." Of significance, besides, are the many joint ventures between A.P. Industrial Development Corporation and private investors: e.g., 204 companies (in 1980–81).

To sum up, there is significant structural heterogeneity in Indian public enterprise; and in aggregate size, it is relatively large. This has a purport for evaluation – on grounds of ownership, sectoral coverage, size and – an aspect not covered statistically above – developmental instrumentality. In line with our theme, the need for C and D levels of evaluation is great. Evaluation of public enterprise in India constitutes a facet of the development strategy of the country.

B. Systemic aspects

Let us start with four high-level quotations.

> Compared to the heavy investment that has been made in these enterprises in the past, the rate of return is very low. The operational efficiency of these enterprises has to be substantially improved in order to obtain a fair rate of return on public investment. (*Sixth Five-Year Plan 1980–85*, p. 62)

> The public enterprises were set up as a result of the conscious policy of the Government to participate in the industrialisation of the country with a view to give impetus to economic growth as well as to achieve certain socio-economic goals. (Bureau of Public Enterprises, *Public Enterprise Survey 1981–82*, p. 1)

The Prime Minister observed at a press conference on 30 December 1983

> that improving the efficiency of the public sector and making it accountable has to be viewed in a broader framework than mere profit-making of the individual units. Certain kinds of production, no matter how unprofitable, are needed if the goal of self-reliance, and the needs of the people are considered. (*Economic Times*, 31 December 1983.)

Stating that the return on capital cannot be taken as "the sole criterion" for measuring efficiency and performance of the public sector undertakings, the Comptroller and Auditor General observes:

> Various socio-economic objectives like creation of employment opportunities, contribution to the national exchequer by way of "duty", provision of housing and urban develop-

ment, export and foreign exchange earnings etc. should also
be taken into account. (Report of the CAG of India: Union
Government (Commercial) 1982 Part I: *Introduction*, p. 38.)

(a) *Levels of evaluation*

The first quotation clearly emphasises the need for the A–level of
evaluation, i.e., evaluation of the managers' performance as reflected in the results of operations. Section (d) below will indicate the
way in which this is pursued in India. Suffice it to say at this stage
that the B–level, which involves a total review of the enterprise,
bringing out the impacts of externalities, of governmental interventions, structured as well as unstructured, and of permanent
handicaps (e.g., unhelpful technologies) does not exist yet. A few
traces of the impacts surface in bits here and there in the CAG and
CPU reports; but no systemic review is made of them. This aspect
is, at times, overshadowed by observations (in the reports) marked, in the words of a critic, by "lack of objectivity, adequate
balance and appreciation of PE problems."[94]

Of crucial value to India would be the C–level of evaluation,
even as the second, third and fourth quotations emphasise the
instrumentality of public enterprise in achieving certain macro
ends. There is yet no clear attempt towards this, as the sections (b)
on substance, (c) on objectives and (d) on agencies – BPE in
particular – evidence. A compelling reason for macro evaluations
of the C–type stems from the alarming state of financial returns.[95]
This must trigger the question: What is the trade-off? Are social
returns that compensate for the financial losses realised?

Equally imperative is the D–level – for many reasons: (i) India
has adopted the path of mixed economy; and public enterprise
represents a pragmatic and non-doctrinaire choice. (ii) Competition is gradually coming to the fore in certain sectors occupied by
the public enterprise, partly accompanied by some reductions in
market imperfections. (iii) Many joint ventures are in progress and
are expected to culminate in progressively fuller assumption of the
concerned activities by private investors, the more so at the state
government level. (iv) Many original investment decisions have
proved wrong in terms of financial and perhaps, in several cases,
social returns. It will be prudent to examine the merits of individual enterprises in today's market and supply conditions.

Hence consistently with the objectives of fast economic growth, institutional characteristics of entrepreneurship ought to subserve the concept of comparative advantage. This term, of course, needs a broad interpretation, so as to comprehend social returns from a given public enterprise as well as the social costs of private enterprise in the given sector.

(b) *Substance*

Without repeating the ideas contained in section 2 of the study, let us look at the major aspects, among others, that warrant evaluative emphasis in the context of Indian public enterprise.

   (i) Many public enterprises (of the central government) are so large and complex in structure that a thorough review of the economies of scale as related to the organisation of individual enterprises is bound to be useful. The constant efforts at organisation reforms and innovations witnessed in Coal India Ltd. serve as evidence in this connection; so does the recent move for the parcelling out of Life Insurance Corporation of India into five parts. The twin questions that the evaluator has to be seized of, are: What is the net economy or diseconomy of a given organisational structure, and what undesirable restrictions on potential competitiveness and managerial growth does it entail?

  (ii) Many public enterprises enjoy high degrees of monopoly power but are not exposed to the scrutiny of the Monopolies and Restrictive Practices Commission. Obvious questions for evaluation would be: whether the price levels and the price structures harbour elements of indirect taxation and cross-subsidisations, whether poor technologies and other managerial inefficiencies are sheltered and whether the long-term interest of the consumer is prejudiced through the enterprise's decisions on the use of net revenues.

(iii) An urgent matter calling for attention on the part of policy makers and the Finance Ministry in particular concerns the losses of capital that several public enterprises have already sustained.[96] These need identification and realistic quantification, so that appropriate policy measures may be taken which will tremendously improve future evaluation techniques.

(iv) The circumstances of top management of public enterprises ought to prompt at least three kinds of evaluation. First, how purposefully and consistently is the technique of functional directorship applied to a given enterprise? Even in the central sector, this is not adequately used in most cases and not at all in several cases. Second, is there a meaningful career development policy in individual public enterprises or over the public enterprise sector as a whole? (Let it not be thought that the Public Enterprises Selection Board ensures this; nor that the creation of a management cadre (on the lines of the Indian Administrative Service) invariably provides for it.) Third, how extensive is the entrustment of top management to non-professional hands – e.g., civil servants on short-term secondment? It is the state government enterprises, as evidenced by A.P., that are heavily marked by the tendency. Fourth – again of greater relevance to state government enterprises – is the chairmanship occupied by a politician or civil servant, active or former?

(c) *Objectives and indicators*

A major systemic gap lies in the absence of objectives in terms of either financial or social functions, a gap which Indian public enterprises share with those in the UK and elsewhere. The Estimates Committee recommended, as early as in 1963, that broad principles regarding the financial and economic objectives of public enterprises be laid down. The Administrative Reforms Commission made a similar recommendation. The Committee on Public Undertakings (CPU) recommended, in 1973, the laying down of macro objectives, both financial and economic, of each public undertaking. Thus there has been no want of expert opinion; but little progress has been made in the direction. As recently as in 1982 CPU observed: "In order to have a proper assessment of efficiency it is necessary to make the objectives and obligations clear to the undertakings. Unfortunately this has not been done yet."[97] Besides, several reports of the CAG contain such comments as: "The objectives and obligations of the Company in terms of the above office memorandum have not been laid down so far (October 1982)," the reference being to the BPE Office memorandum of 3 November 1970 requesting "all Ministers to initiate action to lay down objectives and obligations, both financial and economic, of each enterprise under their administrative control." (Report of the Comptroller and Auditor General of India: Union Government (Commercial) 1981: Part III: *Scooters India Ltd.* (p. 3). Also see 1982: Part II *Rehabilitation Industries Corporation Ltd.*, p. 3.)

The essence of the exercise lies in the determination of the socially desired combination of financial, and identified and quantified social returns in respect of each enterprise.

Probably at the end of long effort, BPE recently produced a document entitled *Performance Aims and Financial Targets of Central Government Public Enterprises 1982–83 and 1983–84*. This contains physical targets of output in the case of each enterprise, by major product, and financial projections. The output targets can have systemic relevance to evaluation if

(i)   they represent an "agreed" product mix;
(ii) they constitute an "agreed" size, inclusive of an "agreed" inventory of unsold or unsaleable stocks; and
(iii) they represent the maximum or optimal output, given a surplus target.

In other words, they should not just represent whatever can be or is planned to be produced, but what is agreed as between the government and the enterprise as the socially desirable output. It is not clear how far this condition is satisfied. The value of objectives as a systemic requisite of evaluation improves proportionately with this condition being satisfied.

The comment applies even more forcefully to the financial projections. These perhaps amount to budget arithmetic. It is doubtful if they have value as "agreed" financial objectives which strictly are derived from "open" governmental transmission accompanied by due notice of Parliament, and if they are exactly analogous to the financial targets set in the UK or to the terms of the "contrat de programme" of France.

A brief comment on performance indicators. Obviously these cannot be devised comprehensively in the absence of agreed objectives and targets. Beyond the level of micro and conventionally formulated indices, which certain annual reports do incorporate, they will be purposeful if only they are so devised as to reflect the accomplishments under desired captions of socio-economic objectives of a given enterprise. It is doubtful if enough exercise is in progress towards this end. BPE's annual surveys do not reflect it.

Volume 3 contains standardised ratios, mostly financial; and one does not get a satisfactory impression on what ought to be or are considered to be the most relevant indicators of performance in each case.

(d) *Agencies*

We shall look at three agencies which have some evaluative significance. Two of these may be considered as distinctive Indian innovations – the Bureau of Public Enterprises and the Audit Boards. As for the third, the Parliamentary Committee on Public Enterprises (CPU), the institution exists in some other countries too; but India merits being bracketed with the UK in point of effectiveness of the Committee.

(1) *The Bureau of Public Enterprises*. This was set up in 1965 as a "nodal staff agency" for public enterprise matters and attained the status of an administrative unit within the Ministry of Finance in 1969. It is under a Director General, currently of the rank of Special Secretary and has nine Divisions (Production, Finance, Management, Information and Research, Construction, Investment and in-depth study, Wages and Salary Administration, Administration and Co-ordination, and Public Enterprise Selection Board Secretariat). The functions are as follows:

  (i) to integrate and strengthen the arrangements for co-ordination and evaluation of all aspects of the management of public enterprises covering technical, economic, financial and managerial policy areas;
 (ii) to provide management consultancy advice to public enterprises and to the ministries;
 (iii) to assist the Public Investment Board in the appraisal of public enterprise investments;
 (iv) to monitor public enterprise performance and report to Parliament, and
  (v) to assist public enterprises in management development.

With a view to monitoring and evaluation BPE has developed an exquisite system of information and evolved a periodic reporting system. Besides, it conducts special duties. It participates in the review meetings of ministries. The claim is made that "it evolves criteria and yardsticks for sectors and individual enterprises, which could be used by the managements of enterprises, the supervisory agencies in government, the Parliament and the public" in the course of a "reliable evaluation of performance."[98]

BPE's concern with evaluation, among its several functions, is reiterated frequently in its reports. The 1972–73 report mentions its object as follows:

> to present Parliament with a total and overall view of the manner in which the investments in the central public sector have been utilised and operated, and also to enable the tax-payer and the consumer to review the overall performance of public enterprise in one single document.[99]

The direction of this object may have been derived from the Estimates Committee's recommendation in 1959–60, in favour of "a separate comprehensive report" to Parliament "indicating Government's total appraisal of the working of public sector enterprises."[100] BPE presents its annual *Public Enterprises Survey* "as an overall review of the physical, financial and socio-economic performance" of (most of) the central government enterprises.[101]

The Annual Report (or Survey) of BPE consists of three volumes. The first gives an over-view, sectorally consolidated (financial) information and an elaborate part containing a statistical narrative on investment, internal resources, inventories, pricing policy, capacity utilisation, ancillaries, international operations, personnel policy, salary structures and industrial relations, cost control and internal audit, socio-economic and welfare measures, and regional development. Volume 2 gives detailed information, enterprise-wise; and volume 3 presents the annual financial statements of each enterprise along with a page of standardised ratios (excerpted in Appendix 2 at the end of this section).

BPE is obviously a multi-purpose agency. It has value in four directions: in establishing a full data base, in offering guidelines representing some uniformity in the approach of multiple agencies within government, in monitoring the operations of the enterprises, and in evaluation. Undoubtedly the information that BPE releases in its reports nearly comes at the top, on international comparison, in public enterprise parlance. This (even if financial) disclosure would be of great value for the evaluator. It is difficult to appraise the efficiency of its monitoring function except in broad terms, viz., that this is basically a parent-department function and that its own involvement could range, at random, over three possibilities – standardised approach, intervention, and healthy scrutiny. None of these is, strictly, evaluation, as earlier sections of our study show.

It is on BPE's role in evaluation that we shall make a few comments.

First, as a government agency it has limitations in so far as evaluations at levels B, C and D are concerned. This is at the root of several of the comments that follow. BPE, understandably, would prefer not to antagonise the administrative ministries, from which there has been "needless intervention . . . in matters that are clearly within the autonomous jurisdiction of public undertakings," as per CPU's findings.[102] BPE is inherently inhibited in full-scale B–level evaluations.

Second, its techniques of information processing and narrative show what has happened, what has been earned or what changes have taken place in various respects over the past years. These do not adequately respond to the essence of evaluation, touching on whether what could have been achieved has been achieved, whether what has been achieved is what society has desired to be achieved, and whether what has been achieved has been achieved (approximately) at the minimum cost or with maximum efficiency.

Third, the information and ratios thrown out by BPE are essentially financial. These are useful but the data for evaluation would be far superior if it were to promote work on performance indicators specific to individual enterprises and include them in volume 3. Over time these are likely to prompt public agencies to bestow thought on their propriety vis-a-vis evaluation of individual enterprises; and one can hope that the right kind of performance indicators will eventually emerge.

Fourth, the most serious point is that the BPE appraisals fall short of the "socio-economic" evaluations that they are expected to be. The teeth of evaluation in public enterprise lie not only in appraisals of financial returns but in critical appraisals of social returns and, importantly, in analytical appraisals of the balance between the two. It is doubtful if a BPE-type agency is the right one for this socio-economic function. A few comments on the reports as of today supply some food for thought on this question.

The general approach is one of factual presentation, without the aid of a perspective in which to evaluate. For instance, there is a detailed compilation on the generation of internal revenues. But how do we evaluate the figures, beyond finding that this year's figure is higher or lower than last year's?

The comment applies to the narratives on managerial practices such as inventories and on capacity utilisation.

It is on the "social returns" aspects that the narrative is particularly of limited utility as an exercise in evaluation. It speaks of encouragement to ancillary industrial units by public enterprises. But what we need to know is: at what cost to them and to society? Could this be lower, and in which cases has the encouragement been of doubtful value?

Similarly, the narrative on export earnings does not throw light on what happen to be the relevant questions from the angle of evaluation, viz., how precisely has the public sector status of given enterprises contributed to the export earnings, has the export–potential been gained through price reductions – if so, at what cost have the export earnings been accomplished, were these exports at the cost of any priority domestic markets and, if so, is the trade-off a socially agreed positive figure?

The statement of socio-economic and welfare measures leaves unanswered many similar questions. Additionally, what are the relative merits of what public enterprises have done, in the context of an overall budget strategy of social welfare; do their activities aggravate dualism in the social structure, and how acceptable is this considered to be at public decisional levels?

The chapter on balanced regional development, by tabulating the distribution of public enterprise assets and labour state-wise, leaves untouched the crucial elements relevant to evaluation on the relative social merits of these facts, the direct financial costs involved, and the net burdens of these on the public exchequer.

Perhaps all this cannot be expected of BPE; and the proper media of evaluation in these respects should be outside of BPE, even non-departmental in structure. To conclude: it is difficult to concede the following claim of BPE vis-a-vis evaluation:

> While the objectives are multi-dimensional and vary in their relative importance at any given point of time, *the presentation takes note of the following aspects*:
>
> (i) whether the public sector enterprises have been success-

ful in capturing the commanding heights of the economy and in sharing the burden of the country's industrialisation programme;

(ii) whether the public enterprises have given an adequate return to the nation on the investments;

(iii) whether the public enterprises have generated additional employment and also helped in protecting employment in cases of sick industrial units taken over from private sector;

(iv) whether the public enterprises have promoted balanced regional development of the country; and

(v) whether the public enterprises have helped in the development of ancillary industries, small scale units, etc.[103]

(2) *The Comptroller and Auditor General.* India has long experience with CAG audit of public enterprises. It has gradually sought to expand from the traditional "regularity" audit to "propriety" audit. A significant step in the process consisted of the establishment of the Audit Board device in 1969 (consequent on a recommendation from the Administrative Reforms Commission), working within and under the control of the CAG. It aims at "undertaking comprehensive appraisals of the working of the government companies and corporations."[104] The Board meets in "groups," each consisting of a chairman and two whole-time members belonging to the Indian Audit and Accounts Department and appointed by the CAG, and two part-time members appointed by the government with the concurrence of the CAG. These two are chosen for their expertise in relation to the enterprise covered by a group. The twin facts – that a specific Board meant for an enterprise conducts the audit and that it is so composed as to cross-fertilise the internal accounting talent of the CAG officers with broad-based external talents – are the commendable features of this unique method.

The CAG's coverage, though extended from time to time, is exclusive of enterprises in which the government or government enterprises hold less than 51 per cent shares, corporations whose Acts do not provide for it – e.g., Reserve Bank of India, Industrial Development Bank of India, Life Insurance Corporation, and the nationalised banks – and certain enterprises like State Bank of India and Industrial Finance Corporation (whose ownership rests with other statutory bodies).

The Audit Board's coverage of enterprises is relatively small – e.g., eleven only in 1981–82. (The BPE enterprises were more than 200 in number.) Five reports were submitted to the government for presentation to Parliament, besides three relating to the previous year.

These quantitative qualifications apart, let us look at the "evaluation" element of the Audit Board reports from the broad angle of our study.

The CAG's annual reports come in several parts, ranged over four captions:

1. Introduction.
2. Results of the comprehensive appraisals of the selected enterprises conducted by the Audit Board.
3. Résumé of the company auditors' reports under directions of CAG and that of comments on the government companies' accounts under Section 619(4) of the Companies Act.
4. Miscellaneous topics of interest in the audit of enterprises not taken up for appraisal by the Audit Board.

(a) The "Introduction" contains valuable and expertly processed financial data on every enterprise (in its Annexe C). The "highlights" on aggregates are recorded separately for government companies, general insurance companies, and statutory corporations. The highlights range over 38 statistical items in the first case, 18 in the second and 25 in the third. Except for the rather homogeneous group of insurance, the *aggregates* by themselves have rather limited meaning in the case of companies and corporations, whose mere commonality lies in governmental ownership. (Item 37 in the case of the companies is sectoral – on the working results.) Useful narrative follows on profits and losses, returns on capital, rates of growth, value of production, cost trends, sources of funds, inventories, consumer composition, ratio of sales to capital, township costs, utilisation of capacity etc. On the whole, the findings are statistically descriptive and in many cases "aggregated" in one way or another.

(b) The unique results of the Audit Board appraisals appear in several parts. A close reading of these reports – e.g., on Rehabilitation Industries Corporation Ltd., and Scooters India Ltd. issued in 1982 – suggests that they contain a superb factual analysis commanding high veracity. Viewed from the angle of evaluation, they seem to be rather limited to incorporating views of "others" – a BPE Committee or the management or the ministry – and to presenting facts and relevant circumstances "attributed" by management etc., on several important issues like non-viability, losses and capital restructuring. Several of the issues raised in section 2 of our study are not covered – e.g., the organisational structure, the economies of size, locational economies, and monopoly and effects. More importantly, the appraisal does not go beyond level A, i.e., beyond stating many bits of relevant data helpful in forming an opinion on the performance of the managers as reflected in the year's operations. The part dealing with the company auditors' reports particularly evidence a series of lapses in internal management and accounting.

The Audit Board appraisals do not touch on the macro impacts on enterprise performance as a whole. They do not deal with any appraisals of the social returns realised and expected. And they do not raise questions of comparative advantage. In other words, the Audit Board's appraisals do not cover the B, C and D levels of evaluation but help in providing relevant material for evaluation at the A–level. Of course, this can be of use to the Committee on Public Undertakings.

In one sense, these comments might not be fair; for more may not be expected of the CAG institution whose supremacy rests on factual findings rather than on evaluative judgements. The latter depend on objectives set or not set but inferred, and social preferences set, or not set but inferred, and might lead the CAG into controversies that could affect the very eminence and credibility of the institution.

One further comment. The inclusion of two non-CAG experts (mostly from top business experience) does not go far enough to ensure the systemic requisites for a comprehensive evaluation ranging over all levels A to D. And it is not clear how involved they tend to be in the whole exercise and whether they go beyond confining their inputs to and from the stage of the CAG staff's basic findings.

(3) *The Committee on Public Undertakings.* This was set up in 1964

with members from the Lok Sabha and from the Rajya Sabha, i.e., from both Houses of Parliament, with the following functions:

(a) to examine the reports and the accounts of the public undertakings;

(b) to examine the reports, if any, of the CAG on them;

(c) to examine, in the context of their autonomy and efficiency, whether their affairs are being managed in accordance with sound business principles and prudent commercial practices; and

(d) such other functions vested in the Public Accounts Committee and the Estimates Committee in relation to public undertakings as are not covered by clauses (a), (b) and (c) above and as may be allotted to the Committee by the Speaker from time to time.

But it shall not examine and investigate any of the following matters, viz.,

(i) matters of major government policy as distinct from business or commercial functions;

(ii) matters of day-to-day administration;

(iii) matters for the consideration of which machinery is established by any special statute under which a particular public undertaking is established.

The terms of the Committee have a focus on the business efficiency of the enterprise and can accommodate not only the A–level but the B–level of evaluation. In fact by virtue of its constitutionally supreme position, the CPU can greatly help to bring out the impacts of non-managers on the managers' performance and on the results of the enterprise as a whole. In practice, however, it is not certain that this has been done in adequate measure, though references do occur in some reports to select areas of governmental interference – e.g., appointments, contracts, and extravagant expenditures.

Social–returns evaluations and adjudications on comparative advantage are not a strong point of the Committee. These depend not only on technical expertise but on knowledge of the government's social preferences and their integrated quantification. There can, however, be an advantage, if and when the Committee makes an excursion into such areas; the government will have to face the conclusions and come out with views on the substantive issues involved. It will be helpful too if CPU can provide well-processed material on how the "actuals" compare with the premises of project evaluation at the level of the Public Investment Board at the time of investment decision. This can certainly be illuminating.

One limitation is that the evidence elicited by the Committee is not published, unlike in the UK. We do not have the opportunity, therefore, of understanding the anatomy of the interface between the managers and the government or between the enterprise and the "externalities," which may have come out in the evidence sessions.

C. *Conclusion*

The country's stake in public enterprise performance is so substantial that a programme that meets the systemic canons of analysis presented in this study is likely to be not only fruitful but essential. It will be ideal to set up a non-departmental agency which may be called a Public Enterprise Commission, with the following functions vis-a-vis evaluation:

  (i) to assist in the formulation of objectives, targets and performance indicators of individual public enterprises;
 (ii) to facilitate the comprehensive conduct of evaluation at all levels (A to D), i.e., evaluation of managers, the enterprise, social results and comparative advantage; and
(iii) to function as the strategic focal point in devising and organising, on its final responsibility, the expert processes of evaluation at the different levels.

It is not to supersede any of the existing governmental or parliamentary agencies concerned with public enterprises. Its chief remit – in the field of evaluation – is basically such as is not, and is unlikely expertly to be, fulfilled by the BPE, the CAG and CPU.

It is not difficult to anticipate criticism of the idea of the Indian context of the civil servant having long entrenched himself in the directoral and management aspects of public enterprise: for example, (a) that the PE Commission will be "one more agency;" (b) that it is too articulate in conception; and (c) that it may not solve the whole problem.

Briefly the answers are: (a) that it will be a helpful and non-duplicatory agency; (b) that the problem is so complex that a conceptually sound agency like this is necessary; and (c) that it can at least be a correct step in the right direction but that it can only succeed if it is allowed to function in a genuine manner.

One last point. The PE Commission will be a friend of public enterprises and an instrument in appraisals of national development strategies.

NOTES

1. Eighth Report from the Industry and Trade Committee (Session 1981–82), *The Post Office* (London, 1982), p. ix.
2. CAG's *Memorandum on The Monitoring and Control Activities of Sponsor Departments of Nationalised Industries*, Committee on Public Accounts, Session 1982–83, p. 9.
3. The Monopolies and Mergers Commission, *National Coal Board*, Vol. 1 (Cmnd. 8920, London, 1983), p. 371.
4. Second Report from the Transport Committee, Session 1982–83, on *The Serpell Committee Report on the Review of Railway Finances* (London, 1983), p. vi.
5. Fifth Report from the Industry and Trade Committee (Session 1981–82), *The Post Office* (London, 1982), p. xix and p. 66.
6. As cited in *The Nationalised Industries* (Cmnd. 7131, London, 1978), p. 19.
7. David Chambers, "Corporate Plans as Commitments," in *Public Enterprise and the Developing World*, Ed. V.V. Ramanadham (London, 1984).
8. Even under B I, interventions through governmental memberships on boards are not easy to establish.
9. In this connection an observation I made on the control system vis-a-vis public enterprise remains valid or has improved validity when we substitute the term "evaluation" for the term "control":

   "The fundamental issue of a control (evaluation) system in public enterprise is not that of control (evaluation) of the managers by the government but of ensuring the realisation of desired socio-economic purposes from the enterprises controlled (evaluated); and its real aim is not so much the accountability of the managers as that of the enterprises. The latter implicates not only the managers but the many others in government or public agencies that set (or do not set) criteria for action."

   (Paper on "Control Systems for Public Enterprises in Developing Countries," Seminar of International Center for Public Enterprises, Ljubljana, 1979.)
10. The concept of "comparative advantage" emerges in a unique way in the current trends of reform in Peru. The Divestment Law drafted by CONADE (Corporacion Nacional de Desarrollo) and awaiting approval of the Chamber of Deputies defines five categories of operations eligible to state intervention and provides that "in each case the forming of a state-owned enterprise should be compared against other forms of intervention. This comparison must also be reviewed periodically" (Felipe Ortiz de Zevallos M., "The Case of Peru: An Insider View" at the Conference on "State Shrinking: A Comparative Inquiry into Privatisation,"

Austin, March 1984).

11. For instance, the Sudanese Government would "consider phased disinvestment in public sector enterprises on a selective basis." (*The Six Year Plan of Economic and Social Development 1977/78–1982/83*, Vol. 1 (Khartoum, 1977), p. 48).

12. Working Party on Government Expenditures, *Report and Recommendations* (Nairobi, 1982), p. 43.

13. *The Nationalised Industries* (Cmnd. 7131, London, 1978), p. 20.

14. The Industry and Trade Committee felt concerned about the impact of the external financial limit on the activities of the Post Office. "The Post Office may raise its tariffs, attempt to contain increases in operating costs or reduce capital spending." "The Government's financial policy towards the Post Office is the main factor in delaying and reducing the investment programme."
   (Fifth Report from the Industry and Trade Committee (Session 1981–82) *The Post Office* (London, 1982), pp. ix, xi.)
   The Industry and Trade Committee's observation on the Ravenscraig non-closure illustrates the complex, if not subtle, way in which it affects the costs of the British Steel Corporation: "Plants which might have been viable with the closure of one of the major sites will now suffer the penalty of having to bear costs per tonne of steel produced, as a result of lower plant-loading. This aspect of the enhanced operating costs resulting from the Secretary of State's policy will have a direct impact on jobs in plants other than, say, Ravenscraig." (Second Report from the Industry and Trade Committee (Sessions 1982–83), *The British Steel Corporation's Prospects* (London, 1983), p. xiii.)

15. *The Nationalised Industries*, ibid., p. 20.

16. The Monopolies and Mergers Commission, *Yorkshire Electricity Board* (London, 1983), p. 166.

17. For instance, the Industry and Trade Committee felt that the five per cent reduction required in the real unit cost of the Post Office over 1981–82 to 1984–85 was a "sharp reduction" requirement. "The Department should consider easing the RUC objective until the level of economic activity, and hence the demand for total services, is more firmly established." (Fifth Report, *The Post Office* (London, 1982), p. xiii.)

18. To cite an instance, the following is a statement of the Department of Energy's responsibilities vis-a-vis the National Coal Board in the UK:

   Department of Energy: Role and Objectives

   The Secretary of State for Energy is the Minister responsible for the operation of the Coal Industry Acts, and the Department of Energy act as the sponsor department for the NCB. The Department have not formally recorded their objectives with regard to their sponsorship of the NCB but my enquiries indicate that these include, within the resources available, the following:

   (a) Advising Ministers on the formulation of the Government's objectives for the coal industry, on policies for the attainment of these objectives, and on questions arising out of the Government's interest in the strategies and key decisions of the industry.

   (b) Assisting the NCB in carrying out its statutory duties and in achieving its financial objectives.

   (c) Ensuring that the NCB contains the external financing requirement within the currently approved limit.

   (d) Ensuring that the NCB's medium-term development plans appear sound and conform to Government policies and long-term strategy for the industry.

   (e) Ensuring that the Board operates in accordance with the agreed develop-

ment plans and takes prompt corrective action to restore performance to
plan.

(f) Operating effective systems of financial control over public funds
advanced to and recovered from the Board.

(g) Promoting the development and use of appropriate indicators of
operational and financial performance including forward projections
which will assist in improving efficiency and effectiveness.

(h) Maintaining a thorough understanding of the Board's operations and of
its position and prospects at any time, and monitoring its progress against
agreed plans and limits.

Committee of Public Accounts, Session 1982–83, Minutes of Evidence,
Department of Industry (London, 1983), p. 11.

19. First Report from the Select Committee on Nationalised Industries (Session
1973–74) *Capital Investment Procedures* (London, 1973). "Government has been
far from successful in its self-imposed role, as set out in the 1961 and 1967 White
Papers and commended by Your Committee's predecessors, of exercising its
control publicly and according to well-defined ground rules without interfering
with the management function of the industries themselves" (p. xxxix).

20. These are covered in V.V. Ramanadham, *The Nature of Public Enterprise*, Part I,
"The Concept of Public Enterprise" (London, 1984).

21. Two references may be cited in support. First, the Parliamentary Committee on
Public Undertakings (in India) regretted "that 13 undertakings have not drawn
up recruitment, promotion, discrimination and other service condition rules. Not
all undertakings have a system of recruiting management trainees. Only 40
undertakings have in-house training facilities and in most cases these cater to
mainly junior levels" (CPU Report No. 49 (1981–82) on *Public Undertakings:
Management and Control Systems* (New Delhi).

Second, see A.N.S. Thapa's paper at the Seminar on Performance of Public
Enterprises, conducted at the Nepal Administrative Staff College, Kathmandu,
in January 1984. He terms the public enterprises as particular "culprits" in not
implementing management development.

22. This may be illustrated by data for Brazil. "An increase in capital intensity . . .
since 1966 has occurred in every public enterprise sector. On average, the typical
public enterprise employee was endowed with 3.5 times as much capital in 1975 as
in 1966 . . . . The average capital–output ratio . . . for the public enterprises
examined rose from approximately 2.3 in 1966–1968 to about 5.0 in 1978. On
average, then, these figures also attest to a significant increase in capital intensity
in the Brazilian public enterprises." Thomas J. Trebat, *An Evaluation of the
Economic Performance of Large Public Enterprises in Brazil, 1965–1975.* (Technical
Papers Series – No. 24, Institute of Latin American Studies (Austin, 1980), pp. 9
and 12.)

23. Some recent data on capacity utilisation in Indian public enterprises are as
follows. In 1980–81 46% of the units under production recorded a degree of
utilisation of 75% or more, 26%, 50–75%, and 28%, below 50%. The last category
in fact rose from 21% in 1978–79. (Committee on Public Undertakings (1981–82)
(Seventh Lok Sabha) Forty-ninth Report on *Public Undertakings – Management
and Control Systems* (New Delhi, 1982), p. 1.)

24. For example, the customer composition of 133 central government companies in
India was as follows in 1982:

Sales to government departments	34.5%
Sales to public sector undertakings	19.9%
Exports	6.8%
Sales to others	38.8%

(Report of the Comptroller and Auditor General of India: Union Government (Commercial) 1982: Part I Introduction (New Delhi) p. xiii.)

25. A subtle way in which this can happen may be illustrated with reference to the ordering by the Central Electricity Generating Board of a power station "in advance of need" – Ince B and Drax completion. These were "unusually expensive." The government paid compensation of £50 million for the Drax completion: this "will fall short of the additional costs which arise from bringing forward by several years a capital expenditure of at least £886 million. These additional costs are and will be reflected in the Bulk Supply Tariff, raising the cost to electricity users." (The Monopolies and Mergers Commission, *Central Electricity Generating Board* (London, 1981), p. 292.)

26. David Chambers employs the term "commitments" in the context of a good corporate plan – commitments on the part of the enterprise managers as well as the government agencies concerned.

27. Nationalised Industries: *A Review of Economic and Financial Objectives* (Cmnd. 3434, London, 1967), p. 12.

28. *The Financial and Economic Obligations of Nationalised Industries* (Cmnd. 1337, London, 1961).

29. For example, in the Office Memorandum of 3 November 1970.

30. For example, in CAG Reports on *Scooters of India Ltd.*, *Rehabilitation Industries Corporation Ltd.* and *Tungabhadra Steel Products Ltd.* (1981).

31. The Coal Industry Nationalisation Act, 1946, section 1(1), charges the NCB with the following duties:

    "(a) working and getting the coal in Great Britain, to the exclusion (save as in this Act provided) of any other person;
    (b) securing the efficient development of the coal-mining industry; and
    (c) making supplies of coal available, of such qualities and sizes, in such quantities and at such prices as may seem to them best calculated to further the public interest in all respects, including the avoidance of any undue or unreasonable preference or advantage."

    Section 1(4) of the Act provides:

    "The policy of the Board shall be directed to securing, consistently with the proper discharge of their duties under sub-section (1) of this section,–

    (a) the safety, health and welfare of persons in their employment,
    (b) the benefit of the practical knowledge and experience of such persons in the organisation and conduct of the operations in which they are employed;
    (c) that the revenues of the Board shall be not less than sufficient for meeting all their outgoings properly chargeable to revenue account . . . on an average of good and bad years."

32. Hansard, Written Answers, 18 March, 1983 (London).

33. For evidence on cross-subsidisations, see Fifth Report from the Industry and Trade Committee (Session 1981–82) *The Post Office* (London, 1982), p. viii.

34. National Bus Company, *Annual Report* 1982, p. 6.

35. Railways Act 1974 and Direction by Secretary of State (19 December 1974) as cited in British Railways Board, *Annual Report and Accounts* 1981, p. 19.

36. British Airports Authority, *Performance Review 1981/82*, p. 4.

37. With reference to Central Electricity Generating Board (in the UK), Hansard 18 March 1983, Written Answers: Nigel Lawson, Chancellor of the Exchequer.

38. See *Corporate Plan 1983–88*, British Railways Board (London, 1983), p. 17. Some other aims are as follows: "At least 87.5% of trains to arrive within five minutes of booked arrival time. No passenger to stand for more than 20 minutes except by

choice. Peak load factors on the heaviest section of a route of 100%–135% for the various types of rolling stock employed."

39. One of the performance aims settled by the Post Office (in the UK). "Although not formal targets, the current Post Office targets have been accepted as reasonable for the present by the Government." The Memorandum of the Department of Industry, Fifth Report from the Industry and Trade Committee (Session 1980–81), *The Post Office* (London, 1982).

40. One of the performance aims set by the government for British Airports Authority in September, 1983.

41. For instance, Fifth Report from the Industry and Trade Committee (Session 1981–82), *The Post Office* (London, 1982).

42. No wonder, the "Government has decided that the published financial targets should be supplemented by publication of performance targets." (*The Nationalised Industries*, Cmnd. 7131, London, 1978), p. 27.

43. For instance, Felipe Ortiz de Zevallos M. observes that, in Peru, "ministers, instead of determining policies and over-all objectives, prefer to impose decisions in every day operations." Conference on "State Shrinking: A Comparative Inquiry into Privatisation", Austin, March 1984, "The Case of Peru: An Insider View."

44. An interesting illustration may be cited from India, with reference to Tunga-bhadra Steel Products Ltd.

> "While formulating a statement of objectives and obligations of the Company in 1972, the Board had decided that the objective of the Company should be to achieve overall production of about Rs 3 to Rs 3.5 crores in a period of 5 years and to earn a gross profit of 8 to 10 per cent on annual production and a return of 6 per cent on equity capital. While the Company has achieved the desired objective in respect of annual production, the percentage of actual gross profit on value of production (1.31 to 3.70 per cent) has been appreciably lower than the target of 8 to 10 per cent. The return of capital also, after having touched a figure of 15 per cent in 1977–78, slumped to a mere 2.7 per cent in 1979–80." (Report of the CAG of India, Union Government (Commercial) 1981 Part II *Tungabhadra Steel Products Ltd.*, p. 62.)

This extensive excerpt is purposeful in that it raises several questions: (a) Are the objectives unilaterally determined by the board, without the government's participation? (b) Have the different targets been mutually consistent with one another? (c) Which of the targets has priority, if all cannot be achieved?

45. The Department of Industry (in the UK) regard "corporate planning as the central feature of their monitoring process." Seventh Report from the Committee of Public Accounts (Session 1982–83) Departments of Industry, Transport and Energy (*The Monitoring and Control Activities of Sponsor Departments of Nationalised Industries, 1983*) p. ix.

46. *For comments on the diversity of understanding on corporate plans and the degree of governmental commitment that exists in the UK, see the papers by John Heath and David Chambers in V.V. Ramanadham (ed.), Public Enterprise and the Developing World (London, 1984).*

47. The following provisions of the "contrat de programme" between the government and Société Nationale des Chemins de Fer Français (SNCF) (originally dated 1969) are illustrative of the usefulness of the technique.

    (A)   Activities and structure:

        (1) Passenger stopping train services: closure or transfer to roads of 10,000 km of services by 1975.

(2) Reorganisation of other services and facilities: e.g., closure of 5,000 km of merchandise services and withdrawal of 5 million train – kilometres of underutilised express passenger services by 1983.
(3) Introduction of an incentive scheme for employees.
(4) Reduction of labour force by 270,000 by 1973.
(5) Average annual rate of increase of "productivité globale" by at least 4.25 per cent during 1969–75.
(6) State compensation payments.

(B) Financial relationships:

(1) Tariffs: State not to oppose moderate increases necessary to balance the revenue account by 1973/74.
(2) Managerial autonomy necessary for achieving the financial equilibrium.
(3) Investment: level and means of financing fixed; a minimum real return of 13 per cent on investments undertaken to reduce costs.
(4) Adjustments for special burdens.
(5) Progress towards a balanced revenue account; a contingency provision of 100 million francs per annum for the revenue account.

(C) Government transport policy:

(1) To keep competition from long-distance road transport at the then existing level.
(2) Equalisation of infrastructure costs (among competing forms of transport.
(3) Equalisation of rate fixing powers of railways with those of competing forms of transport.

(See Appendix D: Example of a "contrat de programme", in Maurice Garner, *Aspects of the French, West German and Swedish experience of government relationships with public enterprises*, Background Paper 2, NEDO (London, 1976), pp. 61–3.)
48. For a review of the practical problems encountered in the working of the contracts, see Diana Green, "Government and Industry in France: a contractual approach," *Public Money*, Vol. 2, No. 2, Sept. 1982.
49. The Monopolies and Mergers Commission, *National Coal Board* Vol. 1 (London, 1983), p. 370.
50. For instance, the Department of Transport found it "impossible to set performance aims which made sense for the railway business as a whole, because the outputs of the business were so varied."
51. It is interesting to cite the Monopolies and Mergers Commission's observation that "the National Coal Board's principal measure of performance is a measure of labour productivity .... The NCB should also give consideration to devising a measure or measures of productivity of capital which properly reflect its true value." The Monopolies and Mergers Commission, *National Coal Board*, Vol. 1 (London, 1983), pp. 376–7.
52. For instance, "a review of performances indicators in three nationalised industries (Coal, Gas, Rail) for the year 1981–82 suggests that they give little information on performance, except on the loosest definition, and no insight into achievement." S.N. Woodward, "Corporate Planning, Commitment and Public Enterprises," in V.V. Ramanadham (ed.), *Public Enterprise and the Developing World* (London, 1984).
    Also, see Peter Mackie and Christopher Nash, in "Efficiency and Performance indicators: The case of the bus industry," in *Public Money*, Vol. 2, No. 3, Dec. 1982. Referring to the MMC's enquiry into four stage carriage bus operators, they

observed: "The Commission's attempt at the admittedly difficult task of comparing the performance of the four operators must be classed as a failure. Some of the performance indicators chosen by them were inappropriate or ambiguous." (p. 44).

53. Informe Final de la Comision Multisectoral de Empresas del Estado (Lima, 1976), cited in Felipe Ortiz de Zevallos, op.cit.

54. Committee on Public Undertakings, Sri Lanka, *Parliament and Public Corporations* (Colombo, 1983), p. 39.

55. The Monopolies and Mergers Commission, *National Coal Board*, Vol. 1, (London, 1983), p. 1.

56. The Monopolies and Mergers Commission, *British Railways Board: London and South East Commuter Services* (London, 1980), p. 1.

57. For a full account, see Brian Branch, *Public Enterprises in Peru; the Perspective for Reform*, Institute of Latin America Studies, Austin, 1982.

58. See next section for an account on SIGEP.

59. The recent Seminar on Performance of Public Enterprises, in which top executives of public enterprises and senior civil servants participated, recommended to the government the establishment of a Public Enterprise Commission to assist in the formulation of objectives, targets and performance indicators and in the evolution of a comprehensive system of evaluation. The Seminar was held at the Nepal Administrative Staff College, Kathmandu, in January 1984.

60. V.V. Ramanadham, *Public Enterprise in Britain* (London, 1959), Ch. III.

61. The Electricity Council Annual Report 1982–82, p. 13.

62. Such measures do not invariably apply to every public enterprise in the UK. For example, in the case of National Coal Board "no targets have been agreed and published for any of the performance indicators." (Committee of Public Accounts (Session 1982–83), Minutes of Evidence, Department of Industry (London, 1983), p. 14.)

63. Hansard, Written Answers (London, 18 March, 1983), pp. 296–8.

64. Committee of Public Accounts (Session 1982–83), Minutes of Evidence, Department of Industry, Memorandum submitted by the Comptroller and Auditor General (London, 1983), p. 3.

65. Select Committee on Nationalised Industries, 1953.

66. Ibid.

67. Report of the Broadcasting Committee (Beveridge Committee), 1949 (HMSO Cmnd. 846).

68. It is interesting that Herbert Morrison objected to its establishment in the following terms: "I would die for Parliament – I have an enormous admiration for it – but I do not think it is the kind of body to which you could entrust this to the point of alteration of the actual management of a complex industrial concern." (Q. 479 Select Committee Report on Nationalised Industries, 1953).

69. First Report from the Liaison Committee (Session 1982–83), *The Select Committee System* (London, 1982), p. 16.

70. For example, "National Board for Prices and Incomes," Report No. 57, *Gas Prices* (London, 1968), p. 1.

71. Financial Secretary to the Treasury, Hansard, 30 Nov. 1981, Col. 48–49.

72. The Monopolies and Mergers Commission, *Central Electricity Generating Board* (London, 1981), p. 1.

73. The Monopolies and Mergers Commission, *British Railway Board London and South East Commuter Services* (London, 1980), p. 1.

74. E.g. Reports on the National Coal Board, Central Electricity Generating Board, Yorkshire Electricity Board, and British Railways Board.

75. See the report in *The Times* by Martin Dickson, Energy Correspondent, London,

106   STUDIES IN PUBLIC ENTERPRISE

8 April 1982.

76. Second Report from the Transport Committee, Session 1982–83, *Serpell Committee Report on the Review of Railway Finances* (London, 1983), p. v.
77. National Economic Development Office, *A Study of UK Nationalised Industries: Their role in the economy and control in the future* (London, 1976), p. 7.
78. Committee of Public Accounts (Session 1982–83) Minutes of Evidence, Department of Industry (London, 1983), p. 9.
79. First Report from the Select Committee on Nationalised Industries (Session 1967–68), *Ministerial Control of the Nationalised Industries*, Vol. II, p. 534.
80. Parliamentary Control of Expenditure (Reform) Bill, 1983.
81. Committee of Public Accounts, Session 1982–83, Minutes of Evidence, Department of Industry (London, 1983), p. 1.
82. British Steel Corporation, *Annual Report and Accounts 1982–83*, p. 2 (London).
83. Engku M. Anuar, *The System of Performance Evaluation of Public Corporation. A case study of Malaysia with special reference to the Urban Development Authority.* Graduate School of Public and International Studies, Pittsburg, 1979, pp. 197–8.
84. Cited in R.N. Dhungel, General Manager, Nepal Industrial Development Corporation, in "Practical Problems of Public Enterprises" at the Seminar on Improving the Performance of Public Enterprises, Kathmandu, Jan. 1984.
85. The figure rises to Rs 900 million if the Kulekhani project now under way is included.
86. "The private sector will be given the first opportunity of promoting the development of industry through investment. Only if the private sector does not respond to meet the investment programme, HMG/Nepal and agencies of government will intervene by way of public investment. Even under these circumstances, HMG will pursue a policy of disinvestment in favour of the private sector as and when the climate for this appears to be appropriate. As principle, HMG/N will not establish industrial enterprises under its own ownership except when large-scale investment is involved and private sector investment is inadequate." "Industrial Policy–1981," Prashasan, *The Nepalese Journal of Public Administration*, July 1983.
87. Resolution No. 1(3)/79–Re-org., Ministry of Production, 22 Dec. 1979.
88. Maj. Gen. (Retd.) Syed Ali Nawab, Chief, EAC, "Monitoring and Performance Evaluation of Public Enterprises in Pakistan," at Seminar on Evaluation of Public Enterprises and Social Responsibilities of Public Enterprises, Islamabad, 1983.
89. Speech of Secretary-General-in-Chief, 2 Sept. 1977, Pakistan.
90. Bureau of Public Enterprises, *Public Enterprises Survey 1981–82*, Vol. 1 (New Delhi, 1983), p. 137.
91. BPE, ibid., p. 137.
92. Detailed data on central government companies for 1980–81 are as follows:

EQUITY INVESTMENT (IN CRORES OF RS.)

No. of companies (1)	Central government and companies (2)	State governments (3)	Private parties (4)	Total (5)
126	91,15	–	–	91,15
15	2,15	16	–	2,31
16	41	2	20	61
9	1,65	6	6	1,77
%	99,5	0,2	0,3	100

Source: *Report of the Comptroller and Auditor General of India: Union Government (Commercial) 1982 Part I: Introduction* (New Delhi, 1982), p. 5.

93. BPE, ibid., p. 139.

94. Laxmi Narain, *Principles and Practice of Public Enterprise Management*, (New Delhi, 1980), p. 265. The reference is to the CPU Reports of the Sixth Lok Sabha.

95. "The net loss of central government public undertakings covered by BPE Annual Surveys" went up from Rs 74.24 crores in 1979–80 to Rs 182.01 crores in 1980–81." (Committee on Public Undertakings (1981–82) (Seventh Lok Sabha), Forty-ninth Report on *Public Undertakings – Management and Control Systems*, p. 49.)

96. To cite from the CAG's Report for 1982 (op. cit.): the cumulative losses of 34 central government companies (Rs 17.11 crores) exceeded their paid-up capital (Rs 7.14 crores) (p. 16).

97. Committee on Public Undertakings, Forty-ninth Report, op. cit., p. 50.

98. *The Bureau of Public Enterprises*, ibid., p. 7–8.

99. BPE, 1972–73, *Report*, Vol. I, p. 1.

100. 73rd Report of the Estimates Committee (1959–60).

101. BPE, 1976–77 Report – Vol. I, p. iii.

102. CPU, Report No. 49 (1981–82), op. cit., p. 52.

103. BPE Survey 1981–82, Vol. 1, p. 2.

104. *Report of the Comptroller and Auditor General of India*: Union Government (Commercial) 1982, Part I, Introduction, p. v.

APPENDIX 1

OPERATING AND FINANCIAL INDICATORS/RATIOS

Sales

Cost of goods sold as percentage of net sales
Net sales as percentage of total inventory
Increase/decrease in sales over prev. year   %
    Price variance   (%)
    Volume variance   (%)

Cost of Production

At current prices
At constant prices of 1977–78
    Increase/decrease in production index   (%)
    Increase/decrease in production cost w. avg.   (%)
Material cost: cost of production   (%)
Manpower cost: cost of production   (%)

Personnel

Number of employees
Average capital employed per employee   (Rs.000)
Average monthly emoluments per employee   (Rs.000)
Average monthly sales per employee   (Rs.000)
Value of production per man/month   (Rs.000)

Inventories

Inventory turnover
Finished goods net sales   (%)
F. goods inventory in terms of no. of days, net sale
Raw material inventory (terms: days,
consumption)

Profitability Ratios

  (i)   Gross profit ratio   (%)
  (ii) Return on investment   (%)
  (iii) Return on equity   (%)

Solvency and Liquidity Ratios

Debt: equity ratio   (%)
Current ratio
Quick or acid test ratio
Asset turnover
Return on asset   (%)
Net profit margin   (%)

Dividend

Cash   (%)
Bonus shares   (%)
Right shares issued

Break-up Value per Share (Rs.)

(Experts Advisory Cell, Pakistan, *Annual Report 1982–83, Vol. II*, Islamabad, 1984.)

APPENDIX 2

MANAGEMENT RATIOS

General

Capital employed (Rs in lakhs)
Value of production (Rs in lakhs)
Value of production: capital employed   %
Cost of production (Rs in lakhs)
Material cost: cost of production   (%)
Manpower cost: cost of production   (%)
Value added (Rs in lakhs)
Value added: capital employed   (%)

Sales

Cost of sales (Rs in lakhs)
Cost of sales: net sales   (%)
Net sales: capital employed   (%)
Net sales: current assets   (%)

Personnel

No. of employees (other than casual)
Average capital employed per employee   (Rs.)
Average monthly emoluments per employee   (Rs.)
Value of production per man/month   (Rs.)
Value added per man/month   (Rs.)
Average monthly sales per employee   (Rs.)

Inventories

Finished goods: net sales   (%)
Work-in-progress: cost of production   (%)
Finished goods inventory (in terms of no. of days' sales)
Raw material inventory (in terms of no. of days' consumption)
Work-in-progress inventory (in terms of no. of days' cost of production)
Sundry debtors (in terms of no. of days' sales)

Financial

Gross margin: capital employed   (%)
Gross profit: capital employed   (%)
Gross profit: net sales   (%)
Profit before tax: net worth   (%)
Net profit: paid-up capital   (%)
R&D expenditure: net sales   (%)

(Bureau of Public Enterprises, India, *Public Enterprises Survey*, 1982–3, Vol. 3 (New Delhi).)

PART TWO

Capital Structures of Public Enterprises

INTRODUCTION

There are at least three reasons why an in-depth discussion on this subject seems to be purposeful. First, the capital structures of public enterprises are, by and large, not the product of market discipline but owe to a degree of deliberate decision on the part of the concerned agencies in the government. It is therefore appropriate that we probe into the policy aspects of public decision (or indecision) in this field. Second, the capital structures have, through their results governed by institutional conventions, an impact on the public exchequer and, consequently, on the government budget. It is therefore helpful to examine how things ought to stand in respect of public enterprise contributions to the government. Third, some public enterprises operate in areas where private enterprises also operate; besides, a large number of mixed enterprises have been emerging, in which public and private shareholders assume joint ownership of the capital. What this development implies for the capital structures is one further question worth discussing.

I shall proceed with my analysis under two broad heads: equity and loan capital, and reserves. Below the surface of these familiar terms arise such other issues as profit distribution, bonus shares, real costs of public enterprise operations, governmental subsidies and capital write-offs. Besides, the degree of relevance of the private corporate–sector analogy will come in for close scrutiny at several points.

Two apparently related issues are kept out of the present analysis, viz., the criteria of investment and the procurement of capital, except for marginal comments on their impacts on the capital structures. Further, the study is neutral to the propriety of the term "profit" and its significance in public enterprise.

One more prefatory submission. The direction of the study is analytical, not empirical. The limited introduction of empiricism in the discussion is merely intended to provide some illustration and clarity to the points at issue. Closely allied to this is the important qualification that, though a large mass of financial data of public enterprises in Pakistan and India have been used for drawing some statistical support for the arguments or findings, the intention has not been to pass any judgement on the profitability or otherwise of the enterprises. Even where a poor financial performance seems to stand out, our purpose is to pursue its implications, particularly of the macro kind, and not to criticise it. In fact the poor results may have been planned at public instance in some cases.

1

Equity and Loan Capital

A word on definitions at the outset. Equity is that part of the share capital which does not carry a guaranteed dividend, unlike preference share capital, is ordinarily irredeemable and ranks for a flexible rate of dividend, which could be zero too. (The term used in the UK nationalised industries is "public dividend capital".) "Loan," in the present context, refers to the long-term borrowings – analogous to the term "total fixed liabilities" used in the publication *Government Sponsored Corporations*, issued annually by the Government of Pakistan, and to "loans" cited in the balance sheets included in *Public Enterprise Survey* (1981/82) of the Bureau of Public Enterprises (BPE) (India), Vol. 3. Here we do not enter into a discussion of whether working capital requirements constitute a part of the figure of long-term loans.[1] A certain share of it usually does. An allied question: is short-term financing, rolled over in perpetuity, to be treated as part of long-term loans?

An accounting principle that is fundamental in distinguishing equity from loans is that in the latter case interest, when such an obligation exists, is charged to the profit and loss account at a pre-fixed rate, whether it is actually paid out in cash or not; whereas in the case of equity the dividend is treated as an appropriation of profit and charged to the profit and loss appropriation account. In corporate parlance there are two differences, viz., that the loan givers, barring an exceptional arrangement, have no rights of direction or management, unlike shareholders; and that while the accrual of interest as a debit to the profit and loss account and as a cost item is automatic (except in the case of an interest moratorium which, not infrequently, characterises several government loans to public enterprises), a dividend is due for payment only when the board of directors recommends it and the annual general meeting resolves in its favour.

A. THE EQUITY–LOAN RATIO

The equity–loan ratio is a shorthand expression of the way in which the enterprise makes up its (external) capitalisation, partly with equity funds and partly with loan funds. The ratio is discretionary, once the relevant legal provisions are met: for example, enterprises cannot be registered under the country's Companies Act exclusively with loan capital; a public corporation Act may constitute an enterprise with loan capital only (as most nationalised industries in the UK illustrate); the government may proclaim guidelines on the equity–loan ratio; and an international agency like the World Bank may propose a given ratio in a specific situation that concerns it as a lender.

Three issues underlie our discussion: (i) what is the significance that attaches to the equity–loan ratio in the corporate sector; (ii) how materially is this qualified in the case of public enterprises; and (iii) what are the macro consequences of a given ratio?

B. THE CONCEPT AND THE QUALIFICATIONS

(a) The minimal paramountcy of the equity component stems from the fact that the relative size of it instils confidence in potential lenders. The higher the equity, the stronger the fall-back for the lenders in case of financial hardship or bankruptcy; and the greater the prospect of the enterprise raising loan funds for its investment expansions. (In practice, the figure that lenders look at is the total of equity capital and free reserves, which is sometimes termed as shareholders' total equity. During times of inflation the actual reserves represent an understatement if the assets are not duly revalued. The issue of asset-revaluation under inflation is still controversial in many countries and is not examined here.)

The practical significance of this point is limited in the case of public enterprises in many countries, for three reasons.

First, most of the loans are derived from the government itself or from public sector financial institutions;[2] and it would be meaningless for the government as lender to look, for confidence, at the equity provided by itself. What ought to be fundamental as a determinant of governmental injection of funds into a public enterprise is, not the structure of its capitalisation, but the substantive feasibility of the investment project.

Some illustrative data on the predominance of government loans among all long-term loans raised by public enterprises are cited below.

In the case of the Indian central government enterprises (covered in the BPE reports), 70 per cent or more of the total loans come from the government (and public holding companies) in the following sectors: "under construction,"[3] steel, minerals and metals, coal, chemicals and petroleum, heavy engineering, medium and light engineering, transportation equipment, consumer goods, trading and marketing services, tourist services and Section-25 companies – 124 out of a total number of 166 enterprises covered by the source tables. In the aggregate 73% of the loans came from the government (1981–82). A break-down of the loans figures by source is not, generally, available in Pakistan's *Government Sponsored Corporations*; but such instances as Larkana Sugar Mills and Investment Corporation of Pakistan indicate the importance of government, among total, loans. In the UK domestic loans are derived from the National Loans Fund; and the White Paper of 1978 emphasised that the nationalised industries should fit in the government's own borrowing strategy.

Second, many of the loans derived from non-government sources (domestic or foreign) carry a government guarantee – e.g. the borrowings of Agricultural Development Bank of Pakistan from the State Bank of Pakistan under the guarantee of the Federal Government; and the borrowings of Kenya Railways Corporation from foreign lenders. Several loans raised by National Coal Board in the UK "are covered by Treasury guarantee both as regards capital and interest payments."[4]

Third, it is rare that a public enterprise is allowed to go bankrupt. Correspondingly the risk of loss that lenders face is nominal.

(b)   An enterprise making, or hopeful of, very high profits finds it advantageous to go in for loan capital, since it will have the opportunity of declaring large dividends after meeting the smaller fixed commitment of interest on loans. Besides, the high dividend rates will have the effect of raising the share values in the stock markets and they help in adding to its goodwill. An increase in loans rather than equity offers current shareholders the convenience of procuring funds without diluting the dividend rates and without sharing the managerial prerogative with additional shareholders.

None of these points has force in the case of a public enterprise whose equity as well as loans come wholly or predominantly from the same source, viz. the government.

There is one qualification, however. Where an enterprise makes a high profit and the government wants to receive a large part of it, equity offers the convenience of dividend declarations of the size desired; and no other device or control instrument is necessary. Loans, on the other hand, limit the government's revenue expectations to the rate of interest agreed upon.

(c)   An enterprise can find in the equity–loan ratio a flexible tool of resource procurement or contraction,

  (i) where, in the nature of its activities, it is in need of effecting periodic increases or contractions in its fixed capital requirements;
 (ii) where it prefers to economise on the financiers' claims on its profits by repaying certain amounts of capital; or
(iii) where it is not able to determine accurately, for any reason, the size of its long-term needs of fixed capital.

On the assumption that equity cannot be diminished or increased beyond the "authorised" capital, except through elaborate procedures under the relevant corporate laws, emphasis can be placed on wielding the loan component to suit its needs.

This proposition has relevance to public enterprises too. In fact, not to do so might involve them occasionally in excessive possession of funds, acquired under the equity device and not easily reducible, which could lure them into channels of utilisation that might be superfluous or of doubtful financial value.

(d)   "Risk" is a vital consideration that adds to the weight of equity in the ratio. The recent introduction of public dividend capital in British nationalised industries like British Airways, British Steel Corporation, Post Office Giro, Aerospace, and British Shipbuilders – an exceptional measure in a situation, for long, of exclusive loan capital – was justified by the government only in the case of those enterprises that were "expected to be both fully viable and also especially subject to cyclical fluctuations in their returns as a result of their trading conditions and the nature of their assets."[5]

The relevance of equity in a situation of risk simply stems from the convention that, unlike a loan, it does not give rise to a cost of capital that must be met even in a year of little or no profit. When in financial stringency, the enterprise is not constrained to find resources for rewarding the equity investors. But this cannot go on for ever or even for a long period; for the equity investors expect to earn enough in good years to compensate them for what they did not receive during the bad years. In the long run, therefore, equity itself constitutes a resource with a cost tag.

In effect equity is to be considered as a device of cash convenience. It ought not to be considered as a no-cost input, for it has an opportunity cost for the economy as a whole. It is not clear that this aspect of equity is adequately recognised by all sides in the case of public enterprises. Corporate behaviour at the micro level is tempted to be unmindful of it. Several enterprises go on from year to year without being able to pay a dividend; and there is no easy way of estimating from a year's financial accounts what the real costs of the enterprise operations have been. Unrewarded equity operates as a means of suppressing the real costs of the enterprise. The costs are there in terms of debt servicing by the government which borrowed the funds in the first place for investment in the enterprise. But these are not reflected in the books of the enterprise itself; and it is not very likely that the matter attracts due attention of Parliament, either.

Let us draw one illustration from Pakistan and another from India. Bannu Sugar Mills has an equity-loan ratio of 1:0.4 (1980–81) and an accumulated deficit that bears an astronomical proportion (1067%) to the equity capital. This is not the whole cost of the venture. To this must be added the "dividend costs" foregone on equity since inception; but the current accounts, by their very nature, do not reveal this point, nor the extent of the unrevealed costs. An apt example from India is Heavy Engineering Corporation Ltd. which had an accumulated deficit of 170% of equity by 1981–82. To this must be added the "dividend–costs" not met since its inception in 1956, if one wants to compute the total real costs of this venture.

C. CERTAIN IMPLICATIONS OF EQUITY

It would be interesting to enumerate categories of situations in the public enterprise sector, in which the justification for equity is heavily outweighed by its effects of suppressing costs and of entailing unnoticed impacts on the public exchequer.

(i) An enterprise that is subject to a structural change and has a capacity far in excess of need or a capacity not suited to the product mix demanded, benefits, no doubt, from a high equity ratio. But a better solution would be to write off capital and effect a basic financial reconstruction, as in the case of British Steel Corporation and British Railways Board. Then the full impact of the measure is noticed by Parliament and the enterprise gets a new lease of life in which all costs of capital can be met, year after year or over a period.

(ii) An enterprise that is marked by substantial errors in investment decision may be unable to meet its capital costs. Here again capital reconstruction, if not liquidation, is preferable to the equity device.

(iii) A public enterprise may sustain planned losses; that is, the government places certain uncommercial obligations on it, culminating in cost excesses over the prices realised. Equity can window-dress the situation by suppressing costs; but a preferable device would be to account for full costs and aim at a transparent flow of funds from the government to the enterprise, appropriate to the transactions involved. The "Public Service Obligation" payment by the Government to the British Railways Board – of about £900 million in 1982–83, roughly illustrates the point. Incidentally it indicates the possibility that certain social obligations imply more serious financial effects than can be met by an apparently cost-free equity device.

(iv) An enterprise may make losses due to inefficiency, quite apart from the consequences of investment errors. Equity would be a poor remedy in this case.

(v) An enterprise in gestation cannot earn enough profits to meet the costs of capital. Two stages of gestation may be distinguished.

In so far as the period of construction is concerned, the equity device prevents the full capitalisation of the costs of capital not currently met; and the eventual figure of capital outlay that appears in the books will be an understatement, the more seriously the larger the investment and the longer the period of construction. From available Indian data, several enterprises currently under construction have relatively large equity segments – e.g., Nagaland Pulp and Paper Co. Ltd. and National Aluminium Co. Ltd. – and a few have all equity and no loan components of capital.[6]

In so far as the early stages of operations are concerned, equity is not improper, though no "dividend costs" are met for a few years, on the assumption that the costs of capital will be compensatorily met in the later years.

Two difficult questions arise: First, how "long" is the long period over which the costs of capital will be met, hopefully, on the average principle? Second, is thought given effectively to the targeting of high enough net revenue earnings in the "later" years to compensate for the early non-recovery of costs of capital?

To illustrate from Indian data again, Appendix 1 cites the enterprises which merit the focus of these questions. The enterprises included in the Appendix have been in existence for about ten years or longer and have accumulated deficits to the tune of half or more (in many cases far in excess) of the equity capital. Many of them are large in terms of capital outlay, and except for a very few, they are currently loss-making too (e.g. in 1980–81 and 1981–82). Thirteen of them have a loan proportion below one; fifteen between one and two; and in the case of twelve loans are two times (or more) of equity. To recapitulate, these enterprises illustrate, in varying degree, the understatement of capital costs in the books of account, complications regarding their gestation status, and the possibility of planned losses in certain cases of promotional pricing or price freezes. All these cases seem to go beyond the innocent purpose of cash convenience on the part of equity.

Similar data for Pakistan are presented in Appendix 2. There seems to be a larger loan segment, on the whole, than in the Indian list of Appendix 1. However, the equity component in every case merits the comments outlined above.

It would be useful to refer at this point to the capital structure of

National Bus Co. (NBC) in the UK. It consists wholly of loans from the government. With inadequate net earnings in most years and progressively rising interest rates, NBC found itself obliged quite frequently to resort to "further borrowing, often at times of very high interest rates" in order to meet the fixed interest obligations. This would not have been necessary, as NBC claims, if it had been "financed by share capital rather than wholly loan capital."[7]

True, but what should be our conclusions? The cost of resources used is there, whether NBC is able to meet it or not. The loan capital simply highlights it, to the financial inconvenience of NBC, which has been unable to earn adequately ever since its inception in 1969. It is strictly elsewhere that one has to look for a solution of the problem, and not through capitalising it with equity.

An interesting instance of equity being used as a technique of giving cost relief to a public enterprise is provided by Pakistan Industrial Development Corporation set up in 1950. In 1974 it was decided to treat all the "Development Loans" so far given by the government as equity. It is not denied that an enterprise such as this has several social obligations; the comment here is on the equity device in dealing with that issue. (Other instances of loans being converted into equity are Pakistan Television Corporation Ltd., Utility Stores Corporation of Pakistan Ltd., and Mechanised Construction of Pakistan.)

A recent instance from the Indian scene may be cited, of considering equity as a solution to the problem of losses. The Committee on Public Undertakings (of the A.P. Assembly) suggested as follows, with reference to the Indo-Nippon Precision Bearings Ltd:[8]

> Debt–equity ratio of the Company as on 31st March 1978 was 1.5:1. Heavy borrowings for expansion programme, coupled with other unfavourable factors ..., have increased the fixed charges of the Company inter-alia, towards interest. In view of its difficult financial position, the Company requested (August 1978) the Government, A.P.I.D.C. and A.P.I.I.C. to convert loans due to them together with interest into equity capital. The Committee recommend that Government prevail upon the two Companies to agree to the conversion of their loans along with interest into equity to reasonable

extent so that some relief is provided to the Company.

To recapitulate: insofar as the equity element of capitalisation is concerned, the analogy of the private sector does not apply with great force to public enterprise (wholly owned and financed by the government), except as a cash-flow convenience in times of occasional financial adversity. Beyond this, it can have three consequences:

(i)   It can help in understating the real costs of operations, when the enterprise does not earn enough to meet the costs of equity capital.

(ii) It can constitute a channel of disguised subsidisation from the exchequer to the extent it does not earn enough for meeting the costs of equity capital.

(iii) Besides, herein lies a little noticed cost for the public exchequer which continues to meet interest on the corresponding public debt.

D. SOME SPECIAL CASES

We shall defer consideration of the situation of a high-profit enterprise with significant equity, to the last section. At this point let us see what qualifications to our conclusions may be necessary when we turn to a public enterprise in which there is private equity partnership. (Several examples are available in Pakistan: Pakistan Petroleum Ltd. and Pakistan Oilfields Ltd., in both of which the government's share is minor, and Pak Arab Refinery Ltd. and Pakistan International Airways Corporation in both of which the government has majority shareholding.) In such cases it seems reasonable to appreciate the rationale of the private investor's approach to the equity–loan ratio question. He is a risk-taker, unlike a lender, and looks for flexible (high) returns and for capital–gearing. Where a mixed venture is formed and the proportion of private equity is significant, the private-sector analogy of the ratio gains in significance. Of course it is open to the government to introduce a legal provision – e.g. in the articles of association – stipulating a dividend ceiling, provided the private partners agree.

Let us turn next to a public enterprise which can borrow funds from the market and is not tied to the government as source. For example, the IRI Group companies in Italy raise substantial amounts of loans "directly on the market."[9]

In the case of a profit-making enterprise, capital gearing has a distributional implication. If it pays interest at a rate lower than its net profit (before interest) rate, a part of the earnings attributable to the use of the loan capital remains with it for a public sector purpose, being syphoned off from the lenders. If the lenders are assumed to represent the rich sections of society, the distributional implications of the gearing can be real.

It may be recalled that we have kept out of this discussion the sources from which public enterprises should borrow. However, we shall make an observation in passing, relevant to the distributional implications. If these were a conscious consideration in the context of the capital structures of public enterprises, it would be a better idea for the government itself to borrow funds, at lower rates of interest than individual public enterprises could, and take advantage of the prospect of a smaller share of the net earnings attributable to those funds reaching the private lenders and a larger share remaining with the enterprises and with the government (if the on-lending rates to the enterprises already provided for a margin in favour of the government) than would be possible if the enterprises themselves directly borrowed from the market. (Of course, this technique may have costs in other ways, most importantly through the absence of direct market tests for resource acquisitions on the part of public enterprises.)

Let us, finally, think of a market situation in which public enterprises compete with private enterprises. The equity–loan ratio circumstances of the latter tend to have some relevance for the former, even as the UK White Paper of 1978 spelt out, with reference to the nationalised industries offered some public dividend capital: "all these industries are operating in highly competitive international markets."[10] If the ratio proves inconvenient to public enterprises during financially bad times by obliging them to service a relatively high segment of loan capital, unlike in the case of private enterprises in like business, their competitive ability weakens; and they may even be constrained to borrow at high rates of interest in order to meet their inflexible interest obligations. In such cases the case for an equity proportion that bears some relationship with that in the private sector of like units is real.

But two circumstances, in practice, need notice. The first is that in the name of competitive propriety, a high equity proportion may be conceded, but no insistence is placed on dividends approximating in the long run to the costs of such a resource. Second, whatever the loan proportion, the interest charge may prove fictitious if it is not paid but continuously carried forward for reasons of accounting. In either case practice defeats theory and accounting convention; and public enterprises, in effect, tend to present conditions of unfair competition with private enterprises whose financiers are keen on a reward. What is important, therefore, is to deal with the fairness or otherwise of competition that is supposed to exist, and not be content with the capital structure as a proxy.

E. TAX AND BONUS ASPECTS

Two other aspects of the equity–loan ratio merit brief reference. The first is the tax implication. Interest paid on loans is a deductible expense for income tax purposes; correspondingly the tax liability of the enterprise is lightened. As a result either the reserve accumulations or dividend rates are favourably affected. It is therefore likely that profit-raising enterprises prefer to have sizeable loan capital. True, the public exchequer's prospect of tax revenues is adversely affected. But some compensatory action is possible through a demand for a high rate of dividend or for a share in profits.

The point has little relevance to public enterprises that are exempt from taxation – e.g. Water and Power Development Authority (in Pakistan).

The other aspect relates to the area of bonus payments to employees. If the amount of bonus is linked to net profit and the latter is defined as "after-interest" profit, a high loan ratio somewhat deflates the bonus base; and the employees derive smaller bonus incomes than if the equity component were larger. This, however, is just a consequence, and is most unlikely to have been a cause of the high loan ratio.

F. STATISTICAL ANALYSIS

At this point let us turn to the financial data of public enterprises, in Pakistan and India, to see if any clear criteria seem to underlie the evolution of their equity–loan proportions.

The 81 cases covered by Appendix 3–A for Pakistan and the 209 covered by Appendix 4–A for India show the wide spread of enterprises over all ranges of the ratio: between all-equity at one end and heavy loan content (three times equity or higher) at the other. On the whole, the number of enterprises with more loans than equity is higher than those with higher equity than loans in Pakistan, the more so if the five banks with all equity are excluded from the finding; whereas in India the conclusion is opposite. Looking at the highest (1:3 or above) loan range, we find nearly half the total number falling in it in Pakistan, as against a sixth in India.

Let us see if any of several apparently relevant characteristics of the enterprises lends perceptible support for the ratios that prevail.

First, by sector of activity: Appendix 3–A indicates a wide spread of enterprises in Pakistan in almost every sector over the ratio scale; so does Appendix 4–A for India. A small point may be drawn, though, viz., that in Pakistan two-thirds of the industrial enterprises and all three in trade and commerce are within the 1:1 ratio, i.e. they have more equity than loans; while in India relatively large numbers in minerals, agro-based, trading, industrial development (not industry as such), and tourist sectors are similarly placed. As for the more-loan-than-equity enterprises coal, textiles and financial services stand out undoubtedly. (There is a substantive implication worth notice here: coal and textiles are the losing sectors and public enterprises therein have not played on relatively high equity as a cost-suppressing device.)

At this point a statistical feature of the Pakistan data, whose import for the cross-classifications contained in the Appendices cannot be guessed, has to be noted, viz., that except in the case of Federal Chemical and Ceramics Corp. Ltd., National Fertiliser Corp. Ltd., Pakistan Industrial Development Corp. Ltd., and State Petroleum Refining and Petro-chemical Corp. Ltd., figures for individual operating subsidiaries of several holding corporations are not available in the *Government Sponsored Corporations* volume.

Second, has there been any relationship between the size of an enterprise in terms of paid-up capital[11] and the equity–loan ratio? Once again the conclusion is of a wide spread of enterprises in every capital size in Pakistan, vide Appendix 3–B; and the relative predominance of more-loan-than-equity ratios occurs in the smallest and the largest enterprise categories (A and E). While broadly similar, the cross-classification of the Indian data in Appendix 4–B suggests that in the small categories (A, B and C) equity is larger than loans[12] – most conspicuously with A, whereas in D, E, F and G categories the larger–loan cases are relatively prominent. One cannot proceed from this to speculate if the smaller enterprises could not easily borrow; for the lender has ordinarily been the government itself and the loan decision would be a deliberate one.

Third, can we discover any relationship between profitability (as recorded in a recent year) and the loan–equity ratio, attaching to the profitability figure the character of an imperfect proxy for the risk factor as perceived over points of time when capital-raising decisions have been made? The cross-classification for Pakistan, despite a wide spread, produces an interesting result, viz., that the highest–profit[13] enterprises had, all but one, an equity smaller than loan capital (Appendix 3–C). This may illustrate capital gearing in action. At the other extreme, i.e. of loss-making enterprises, a large number have more loans than equity. The Indian data, of Appendix 4–C, do not suggest any consistent relationship as we move from the loss-making enterprises to those making the highest net profit. The 10–25 per cent and 100–200 per cent categories have a high proportion of equity-oriented enterprises while those in between (i.e. 25 to 100 per cent) present the opposite characteristic.

A different version of the risk proxy may be examined next, viz., the rate of gross profit (i.e. before interest and tax) on capital employed.[14] (Data on this figure are available in the Indian volume only.) The conclusion from Appendix 4–CI is similar to the above, viz., a wide spread of most gross profit ranges over the equity–loan ratios, except for the relative concentration of the highest gross–profit enterprises (above 30 per cent) in the below 1:1 ratio; that is, they have more equity than loan capital.

Lastly, do enterprises of different ages present any differences in equity–loan ratios? In other words, has the ratio policy been different from time to time, or have enterprises evolved any noticeable trends of ratio as they have aged? The data for Pakistan on dates of incorporation of public enterprises, as classified in Appendix 3–D, indicate a spread over all ranges of the ratio in respect of all dates of incorporation. This is most clearly illustrated by the large number (57) incorporated during 1970–75. Many of these may have been the product of large-scale nationalisations in early 1970s. From the Indian data contained in Appendix 4–D, it is difficult to infer any clear relationships either, except for the fact that among the most recently incorporated enterprises a high proportion is equity-oriented; perhaps borrowing has not yet been easy or might be more important as they age.

Let us conclude the statistical exercise with an enquiry into how heavy, in relative terms, interest charges have been for enterprises standing at different points on the scale of equity–loan ratio. The measure, found most appropriate within the constraints of data availability, is "financial expenses" as a proportion of total expenses of the enterprise. (These mainly, though not exclusively, represent interest on loans). The proportion is a function of capital intensity as well as the equity–loan ratio. Where both are high, it is naturally high. Appendix 3–E refers to 27 public enterprises in Pakistan, for which the required data have been available (for 1981–82). It suggests that almost all the enterprises with relatively high financial expenses (i.e. above 10 per cent) had more loan than equity capital (in most cases by three times or more); that almost all those with more equity than loan capital had relatively low financial expenses (i.e. less than 10 per cent); and that two-thirds of the enterprises with loan capital two times equity (or more) had relatively high financial expenses (i.e. above 10 per cent). The data confirm the veracity of liquid-cash hardships that enterprises with high loan components can face in times of poor net revenues.

G. LOANS AND TERMS

Before we proceed to the next section (on reserve capital) there is one aspect of the long-term loans of public enterprises which merits a comment in our analysis of capital structures, viz., the exact validity of the terms of loan. Loans offered by the government have various versions: e.g. non-repayable and free of interest,[15] non-repayable but with interest, repayable and free of interest, repayable and with interest; and a moratorium may be attached to interest and/or repayment. As we review the loans picture in different countries, developed as well as developing, we get the impression that adequate thought has not been given by the governments to the following aspects of lending:

(i) Is interest exemption intended to serve as a cost relief designed to respond to some social obligations assigned to the enterprise? And is the loan analogous to equity, except that there can be a dividend on the latter and that the former may be repayable?

(ii) Does the moratorium reflect a reliable calculation as regards the public intention to offer the enterprise a cost relief for a given period only, at the end of which it is expected to fulfil its functions without such public support?

(iii) Where repayment is specified, is it anticipated that the enterprise will be able to raise enough internal resources to meet the loan repayment obligations year after year?

The first two aspects call for difficult costing exercises regarding the social obligations and raise questions of disguised subsidisation. The relevance of the last one can be easily illustrated from experience all over. For example, National Bus Company in the UK has not been able to meet the loan repayment instalments year after year, except from fresh borrowings – again from the National Loans Fund; Kenya Tourist Development Corporation and National Irrigation Board have been unable to repay loans to the government; and so on.

At the level of analysis, the basic question is simple: does the government anticipate that the enterprise will earn sufficient profits to meet all costs, depreciation, interest and also loan repayments? In several cases, e.g. irrigation in Kenya, the prices are set too low under government approval or at government instance even to realise all recoverable costs; and in others a complex question of pricing arises, viz., whether the enterprise should be required to raise prices so as to earn enough for loan repayments. This is possible in the case of strong and inelastic demands, or by accepting ouput reductions that go with price rises. But there are macro implications. Loan repayment receipts by the public exchequer are but one aspect of the matter. There can be disadvantages on grounds of consumption affected; and there can be genuine consumer concerns with what may be described, if not challenged, as a monopoly practice.

It is not our purpose to argue against repayable loans. The point is that the aforesaid implications should be adequately scrutinised before adopting the system.

In fact the repayable-loan technique is commendable on several grounds. First, even if fresh borrowings are simultaneously necessary, the enterprise can be brought under new interest rates that more properly approximate to the market rates than the original ones. Second, the government will be able to practise effectively the policy of rotating its funds in wielding its entrepreneurial initiative in different sectors of activity, instead of finding its resources permanently locked up in a few early lines. Third, the enterprise and the government will both be watchful for any possibilities of contraction or privatisation, consistent with the mixed economy principles of the country; and loan repayments can be an occasion for this. Not that loan repayments are to prompt privatisation, but the two can conveniently go together, when privatisation is decided upon on its own merits. The enterprise can continue to be in the public sector even after offering for sale minority shares to private investors; as funds are thus available under the head of equity capital, the enterprise can undertake loan repayments without prejudice to the aggregate needs of capital. This point is undoubtedly relevant to the current trends of policy changes vis-a-vis public enterprise in several mixed economies, e.g. Kenya, Sri Lanka and Pakistan.

While on loans, let us refer to a strange situation. An enterprise, whose deficits are so large and continuous that it faces an acute cash problem, may be provided by the government with funds to meet it. How are these to be treated? One way is to consider these as a grant meant to meet the deficit – not simply a cash deficit. This is a commendable course, particularly when the deficit is a continuing one and there is no reasonable hope of its being wiped out by profits in the immediate future. The grant correspondingly reduces the accumulating deficit. The other technique is to treat the government's contributions as a loan, carrying an interest rate. This increases the book figure of capitalisition and the loan component. The enterprise is likely to record a larger deficit in subsequent years because of the increased interest obligations. The need for fresh government contributions, termed loans, will arise again and again. Looking at the balance sheet one gets the erroneous impression that capital investment is expanding. The fact is that all the time capital is being eroded. It will be preferable to face the problem of the enterprise logically and effect the necessary write-off representing the loss of capital already sustained. This relieves it of the impossible burden of additional interest charges as well as the fiction of increased capitalisation.

There can be a far-reaching consequence. The equity–loan ratio of the enterprise continuously moves in favour of the loan component and its ability to raise borrowings is correspondingly weakened. If there exists a statutory or conventional equity–loan ratio, the disadvantage for the enterprise can be all the more serious.

The reason why the government adopts the practice of treating the deficit-grant as a loan is probably that it is unable to make a firm determination on its inherent status, namely, that it is just a grant for a revenue deficit. There may be political difficulties in being so categorical. To treat it as a loan may not be immediately problem-raising, but it is building up a major problem of write-off.

H. MISLEADING INFERENCES

We shall conclude this part of the analysis by emphasising the limited relevance of the capital-structure concept in public enterprise, especially in the sense of the equity–loan ratio. Appendix 5 presents a simple arithmetic illustration of how misleading inferences on profit rates in terms of equity capital can be. Enterprises A, B, C and D employ the same quantum of resources and earn the same revenues from the total of resources employed, but the profit rates in terms of equity capital turn out to be quite diverse, because of diversity in the capital structures. (A has very little loan capital, D has very little equity capital, and C has issued bonus shares.) Not much significance attaches to these rates when (i) both the equity capital and the loans come from the government; (ii) shares are not quoted or freely traded in; and (iii) the shareholder is not motivated by gains in the stock exchange. What matters is the rate of return in terms of the total investment, which remains constant in all the cases (see line 10 or 16 in Appendix 5).

2

Reserves

We shall now turn to the implications of reserves in the capital structure of a public enterprise. The reference is to non-specific reserves[16] which represent retained profits. It is generally considered that these reflect managerial prudence in setting aside a part of the net revenues for the rainy day or for investment or any other purposes at the discretion of the board, and that they indicate the successful nature of the enterprise in terms of financial earnings.

A. DIVIDEND INCOME FOR THE GOVERNMENT

The institutional conventions governing the capital structure are such that, while loans earn interest almost automatically and equity earns dividends when declared, the reserve component does not bring in a reward to the government as owner. (True, its use as a resource influences the level of returns.) The larger the reserve, the more serious the non-accrual of a return on this base – as a current flow – to the public exchequer. Of the 84 enterprises of Pakistan for which detailed financial data are available in *Government Sponsored Corporations*, some 57 had reserves in 1980–81; 28 of them (or a third of the total number) had reserves that equalled or far exceeded the figure of ordinary capital. In the case of India, about half of the enterprises covered by *Public Enterprise Survey* had reserves in 1981–82; some 50 of them (or about a fourth of the total) had reserves equal to or far higher than paid-up capital. So the returns attributable to this form of capital outlay but not received by the public exchequer should be substantial in both Pakistan and India in respect of a considerable number of enterprises.

One way in which, under the conventions of the capital structure, this circumstance can be remedied is for the enterprises to take out large proportions of net profits for dividend purposes and declare dividends at such high rates as compensate the government on both equity and reserves. But this does not seem to be happening in many countries; and the data from Pakistan and India amply illustrate this observation. Appendix 6–A indicates that in Pakistan nearly half of the enterprises which had net profit retained all of it in business, and a meagre five took out half or more of it for dividend purposes. Appendix 6–B for India is almost corroboratory in both respects.

Of further interest is the cross-classification of the reserve–sizes and profit retentions. While one may assume that enterprises with relatively small reserves are likely to be inclined to keep as much net profit as possible from utilisation as dividend, those with relatively very high reserves themselves took out miserly proportions of net profits for dividend purposes and practised profit retention in business far more importantly – in Pakistan as well as India.

But this did not imply that the dividend rates on the part of enterprises with the highest reserves (in relation to share capital) were relatively low. Appendices 7–A and 7–B (respectively for Pakistan and India) show the structure of dividends declared in cross-comparison with the reserves structure. On the whole the relative frequency of dividends in the higher ranges (i.e. above 10 per cent) seems to be greater in the public enterprise sector of Pakistan than in that of India. This apart, of the enterprises with the largest reserves (in relation to share capital), nearly half in India and all in Pakistan offered dividends of 15 per cent or more.

Two inferences are possible: to pay dividends that may be considered as reasonably high, it has been enough for the enterprises concerned (particularly for those with relatively high reserves) to draw out relatively small portions of net profits for dividend purposes. And any attempt to utilise more of net profits as dividends would result in the dividends shooting up very high indeed. Just a few sporadic examples exist: National Petro-specialities Division of State Petroleum Refining and Petrochemical Corp. Ltd (in Pakistan): 250 per cent, and Cochin Refineries Ltd (in India): 72 per cent.

In the event, reserves accumulate, the proportion of net profits taken out for remunerating the investor, viz., the government, continues to be relatively low, and the component of capitalisation on which the public exchequer does not receive a reward – in the nature of a current flow – increases progressively. Besides, under conditions of inflation, the real value of reserves, taking into account the case for asset revaluations, exceeds the value stated in the books.

B. A SHARE IN PROFITS FOR THE GOVERNMENT

Let us pause for a critical look at this phenomenon. It is claimed, and correctly, that the accumulating reserves represent an internal resource of the enterprise and an index of strength. While we shall revert a little later to examine whether this is an unalloyed advantage from the macro standpoint, let us first present the point that the public exchequer's merits in looking for a larger share of the net profits arising out of the total capitalisation of a public enterprise are not insubstantial at all. The reasons are as follows:

   (i) The reserves represent de facto re-investments by the government. Instead of taking the lion's share of profits first and then introducing them as fresh investments, the government has, over a period of years, let the resources remain in the enterprise itself. It is logical for the government to expect a reward on this component of investment as well.

  (ii) Many public enterprises have not paid dividends on equity for long periods. When in a position of high profits, they ought to make available profit transfers to the government on a compensatory scale.

 (iii) In several countries governments are running budget deficits and are under severe pressure on economic grounds as well as from international agencies such as the I.M.F. to strive for revenue increases and expenditure contractions in all plausible ways. Public enterprises have to play their due role in offering the public exchequer increased incomes. Or else, the burdens on the general tax payer tend to be severe; and they might represent an utterly inequitable spread, especially where the tax system is regressive.

 (iv) Some of the causes of financial stringency experienced by the public exchequer have a public enterprise genesis. The capital resources provided by the government to public enterprises have for their counterpart, roughly, a corresponding public debt which has to be serviced in terms of interest as well as repayment. If the returns from the enterprises are smaller than the debt servicing costs, the government ends up with a deficit directly traceable to the public enterprise sector. Another similar situation arises in the case of losses of capital sustained by certain public enterprises, as illustrated by the high figures of accumulated deficits in several cases in Pakistan and India – cited earlier – and in many other countries like Kenya, Tanzania and the UK. Write-offs are a logical step in such cases; though they rationalise the financial problems of the enterprises concerned, they entail the continuous incidence of debt-servicing burdens on the public exchequer. The question is how these burdens are to be spread among (i) those enterprises that have been directly responsible for the problem, (ii) all public enterprises, and (iii) the taxpayer in general. The first may be immediately difficult; and the second may have to come in for partial choice, the third being the residual target.

To sum up the argument: profitable public enterprises ought to make available to the government larger amounts than so far passed over through relatively paltry or no dividends. This eats into their reserve potential; and public enterprise executives raise a big counter-argument: "it reduces internal resources." Let us meet this "sacred cow."

To avoid misunderstanding it may be mentioned at the outset that the suggestion is not: not to have reserves; but that a compromise is needed between reserve-building and profit incomes to the government.

First, to let the government receive a larger part of the net revenues of public enterprises than has generally taken place so far, does not negate their chance of receiving the self-same amounts back from the government towards investment. The chance depends on whether the government considers the investment as justified.

This brings us to the second and basic issue, viz., that a rigorous scrutiny of the justifiability of an investment has a better chance of being undertaken when the funds are to be derived from the government (or from an external source outside the enterprise) than when the enterprise has ready access to internal resources. This is a general statement; and there can be exceptions. But one thing is certain: investment decision on the basis of funds to be

procured from the government can never be easier than one
dependent on internal resources; the former is a government-
enterprise decision while the latter can be a board decision, within
limits and in formal terms.

Third, there is bound to be a qualitative change in the focus of
investment decision when the resources first reach the government
and then come to the enterprise. In programming investments of
internal resources the outlook of the enterprise is understandably
limited to the best of the projects possible within its range of
functions. On the other hand, the government, when determining
the investment merits of an enterprise looks widely at the competing demands for the funds from other enterprises as well and
can decide on the best cost-benefit options in macro-economic
terms.

Two other possibilities exist too. The government may decide to
utilise the funds for certain of its social expenditure projects either
in terms of capital expenditures or as recurring expenditures.
Further, there may be occasions, in such fields as agriculture,
small industry and rural welfare, when the government decides
that a specific investment ought to be implemented through the
regular departments of the government for better results rather
than through a given public enterprise. The opportunity for such a
determination would be lacking if the resources just stayed as
undistributed profits and reserves with the enterprise itself.

Fourth, high profits accumulate with an enterprise, in ultimate
analysis, because it possesses and uses monopoly power and because the government approves of its resource-raising prices which
have the effect of an indirect tax on the consumers concerned. The
reason why the consumers of a public enterprise are denied the
chance of lower prices is, again in ultimate analysis, that the
government approves of their being a target for charges far in
excess of the costs of outputs taken by them. These are analogous
to indirect taxation; and it is proper for the government to look for
a share in the incomes raised in this way. Otherwise, it can resort to
an excise duty or a "levy" as in the case of British Gas Corporation
(at 5 pence a therm of gas for 1982–3).[17]

Finally one may add a rather provocative point. Accumulating
reserves can tempt the managements into "conspicuous" expenditures in the sense of over-generous employee benefits and "social
expenditures." Some balance is probable if a system is devised for

moderating reserve retentions through increased profit payments to the government.

C. PROFIT-SHARING METHODS

It may be recalled that high rates of dividend are one means of effecting needed improvements in the government's revenue from public enterprise investments. There are two other ways.

One is to convert a major part of the reserves into share capital through the issue of bonus shares. This is a normal practice in the private sector. It has been done in Pakistan in the case of Trading Corporation of Pakistan Ltd., where bonus shares out of profits (of Rs 92.50 million)[18] were issued so as to make an originally very small share capital far larger. Such a measure permits "current" transfers of a sizeable part of the net profits to the government by increasing the capital base to which a reasonable rate of dividend is applied. And the reserve resources themselves stay in the enterprise – a point that should be pleasing to the managements, though under a different name, viz., share capital. The measure presupposes certain procedural steps, permissive articles of association, high enough or increased ceilings of authorised capital, and board-and-shareholder resolutions.

The other method consists of a straightforward stipulation of profit-sharing between the government and the enterprise. The ratio may apply uniformly to all public enterprises. For instance, Decree–Law No. 21 of 1967 of Syria stipulated, by Article 30: "The profits of each enterprise shall be distributed as follows: 25 per cent to the workers; 75 per cent to the State."[19] To cite a recent instance: In Peru half the post-tax profits of public enterprises were to be transferred to the government; even the other half could be, if the public enterprise could not justify re-investments. (Automatic implementation of this law D.L. 20810 of 1974 was not too simple in practice.)

Or, this profit-sharing ratio for an enterprise may be set on a basis designed to be the most appropriate to its circumstances: as in the case of IRI in Italy:[20]

> The net annual profits ... shall be apportioned as follows:
> 20% towards the ordinary reserve fund;
> 15% towards the fund described under section 24;

the remaining 65% shall be allocated to the State Treasury in repayment of the endowment fund and the sums granted to the Institute by the Treasury. When repayment has been completed, the 65% shall be allocated to a special reserve fund. (Section 17)

The 15% share of the profits mentioned [above] shall be put into a special fund to finance industrial management training ventures and vocational training and social welfare schemes.

Laboratories and industrial and management training courses may be set up and subsidized. (Section 24)

To cite another instance: The Agricultural Finance Corporation Act (1970) of Kenya stipulates, under Section 16, as follows:

As soon as the reserve fund and other funds of the Corporation total such amount as in the Board's opinion is adequate to enable the Corporation fully to carry out its objects, there shall ... be paid to the Permanent Secretary to the Treasury such amounts as the Board shall direct out of:

(a)   the profits of the Corporation; and
(b)   the reserve funds of the Corporation.

The amounts so paid "shall be applied towards the redemption of any loans made by the Government to the Corporation, and interest upon the amount repaid shall cease to be payable as from the date of repayment."

Or a permissive provision may be included in the Act governing a public enterprise (or in the Articles of Association in the case of a government company) such as the following applicable to Industrial and Commercial Development Corporation (in Kenya):[21]

The Minister of Finance may, from time to time, after consultation with the Minister, direct the Corporation to pay into the Consolidated Fund any money held by the Corporation and deemed by the Minister for Finance to be surplus to its existing or anticipated requirements.

An interesting device has been adopted in the UK in the case of a highly profitable public enterprise, the British Gas Corporation. While setting its financial target, the minister formulated it so as to make it more than a measure of profit transfer; it would be treated as a repayment of the outstanding loan in the recent years up to 1980–81 (during which year the external financial limit consisted of a positive cash flow from the Corporation to the government, of £400 million).[22] Of course this method, in principle, can raise a future problem: assuming that all loans are repaid, and that high profits continue to be realised, a new device of transferring the profits to the government has to be found. A straightforward profit-sharing arrangement can be of use.

The formulation of a profit-sharing formula is far from simple. Some major questions are briefly outlined below.

First, a many-public-enterprise situation raises the question of whether there should be a common ratio in which the government and the enterprises share the profit, or the ratio should be diverse among sectors, regions and enterprises.

Second, should the profit-sharing commence beyond a profit-threshold or apply to all profit? In the former case, how is the size of the threshold to be determined? In terms of share capital, aggregate capital outlay, nature of risk borne by the enterprise, or any other magnitude? And should the sharing ratio be constant for all sizes of profit or change progressively or regressively as profit size increases?

Third, if there exists some private shareholding in the enterprise, what impact does this factor have on the profit-sharing principle in detail? Will there be some bias, instead, for a "levy" on output so as to siphon potential profit into the public exchequer before it ends up as profit in the accounts of the enterprise?

Fourth, when an enterprise is known to have admissible needs of investment, should the profit-sharing principle be in abeyance or should the government prefer receiving the income first and offering capital resources later on? The latter may be effected through a book adjustment in accounts.

Finally, the principle ought not to operate so mechanically as to suppress the initiative and pride of the enterprise personnel in raising a profit: nor should it ruin the chances of consumers hoping for price reductions or quality improvements (dependent on investments).

The whole question may seem somewhat academic in countries where most public enterprises are not in a clearly profit-making situation. But the situation is changing. In several countries, both developed and developing, enterprises do exist which raise high profits; and the suggestion on the propriety of thinking in terms of a transfer of some public enterprise profits to the public exchequer by means of a methodical system is not so academic as it may seem. The capital structures of public enterprises as they exist have not been conducive to this; hence the need for bonus share decisions and/or profit-sharing formulae.

3

Conclusion

The broad conclusions of our analysis are that the capital structure of a public enterprise ought not to operate as an institutional device that interferes with the substantive and macro criteria relevant to its operations and that the private sector analogy has severe qualifications.

The component of grants should strictly represent those cost reliefs that the government decides to offer in view of the extra-enterprise (or social) functions assigned to the enterprise; and where there is no more of these to be realised, grants should be suitably converted into equity or loans, assuming that they remain represented by assets. Equity itself should be a device of cash-flow convenience and not a means of a permanent or long term non-recovery of costs.

One of our specific conclusions is that equity capital ought not to be used as a device to deal with loss-making operations or with the impacts of social obligations. The causes of losses call for scrutiny and appropriate measures of amelioration other than the use of the equity device. And social obligations must be accompanied by transparent subsidies from outside the enterprise and not by cost reliefs through the equity device.

The terms of loans should approximate to the market conditions as nearly as possible and any significant deviations should rest on conscious determinations of the social–function costs shouldered by the enterprise. (Whether these should lead to interest–cost reliefs or transparent subsidies is an important question.) Not only should the enterprise earn adequately on all capital employed, including reserves, but its current flows of reward to the government should adequately cover the reserve capital as well.

Public enterprise finances are a part of public finance in many respects.[23] Hence the macro aspects of the capital structures of public enterprises, along with their terms of annual payments to the government, should subserve the interests of the public exchequer equally with those of the enterprises themselves. From this angle several changes in the prevailing capital structures and the terms attached to them seem to be necessary; and these call for competent involvement on the part of accountants, economists, public enterprise executives, and officials dealing with public enterprise.

NOTES

1. In fact where there has been a heavy loss of capital and the government injects a cash contribution into the enterprise in the name of working-capital advances, what really takes place is an addition to the capital outlay, with the difference that the aggregate capitalisation (consisting of the original and these later provisions of funds) is too inadequately represented by assets. This is illustrated by Delhi Transport Corporation (in India), whose deficit in 1981–82 was Rs 2,07 lakhs, as against the fixed capital of Rs 84,23 lakhs; and there was a working capital loan from the government to the tune of Rs 70,26 lakhs. Bureau of Public Enterprises, *Public Enterprises Survey*: 1981–82: Vol. 3, p. 485 (Delhi, 1983).
2. The Italian experience reveals a contrast. For instance, Ente Nazionale Idrocarburi (ENI) received from the government only seven per cent of the funds needed by it in 1981; "The remainder was raised by recourse to the money market." (*ENI, Annual Report 1981*, p. 6) (Rome).
3. That is, enterprises described as still "under construction" in the BPE reports.
4. *National Coal Board, Report and Accounts 1981/82*, p. 60 (London, 1982).
5. *The Nationalised Industries*, Cmnd. 7131 (HMSO, London, 1978), p. 29.
6. *Public Enterprises Survey*, 1981–82, Vol. 3.
7. National Bus Company, *Annual Report 1980* (London, 1981), p. 17.
8. Committee on Public Undertakings (Sixth Legislative Assembly), *Report on the Indo-Nippon Precision Bearings Ltd* (Hyderabad, 1979), p. 5.
9. *IRI, 1981 Annual Report* (Rome), p. 107.
10. Ibid., p. 29.
11. The data for Pakistan refer to "ordinary share capital" (paid-up) as found in *Government Sponsored Corporations*, and, for India, to "paid-up capital" as found in the detailed enterprise-wise financial statements found in *Public Enterprise Survey: 1981–82* Vol. 3.
12. The data on loans refers to the item "total fixed liabilities" as found in the Pakistan volume, and to the aggregate of loans (from the central government, from foreign parties and from others) as found in the Indian volume.
13. Net profit (as per cent of ordinary paid-up capital) refers to profit after interest on loans and before tax in the case of the Pakistan enterprises and to profit after interest and tax in the case of the Indian enterprises.
14. Defined as gross block less accumulated depreciation thereon plus working capital, *Public Enterprises Survey: 1981–82*, Vol. 1, p. 372 (op.cit.).
15. Strictly these are analogous to grants or equity.
16. As illustrated by the term "surplus and reserves" in the Pakistan volume and by "reserves and surplus" in the Indian volume.
17. *British Gas Corporation, Annual Report 1980–81* (London, 1982), p. 8.
18. *Government Sponsored Corporations: 1980–81* (Islamabad, 1982), p. 289.
19. "The Financing of Industrial Enterprises in the Public Sector in Syria" by

Theodore Chadarevian, Director of Research and Planning at the Central Bank of Syria, (Interregional Seminar on Financial Aspects of Manufacturing Enterprises in the Public Sector, Rome, December, 1968).
20. *Statutory Instrument 51* of 12 February 1948, enacted as Law 561 of 17 April 1956 (Rome).
21. *The Industrial Development Ordinance*, Ch. 517, Laws of Kenya (Nairobi, 1962).
22. *British Gas Corporation, Annual Report 1981–82*, p. 9.
23. This theme is examined at some length in Part III of this volume.

APPENDIX 1

ENTERPRISES WITH LARGE ACCUMULATED DEFICITS (1981–82) (INDIA)

Enterprise (1)	Date of incorporation (2)	Equity–loan ratio (3)	Deficit as % of equity (4)	Profit/Loss during the year (5)
Bharat Aluminium Co.	1966	1:0.9	63	L
Hindustan Copper Ltd.	1967	1:0.9	44	L
Indian Firebricks and Insulation Co. Ltd.	1960	1:3.7	279	P
Bharat Coking Coal	1972	1:3.2	191	L
Fertilizers & Chemicals (T) Ltd.	1943	1:0.1	52	L
Fertilizer Corp. of India Ltd.	1961	1:1.3	50	L
Indian Drugs & Pharmaceuticals Ltd.	1961	1:1.1	83–	L
Bharat Heavy Plate & Vessels Ltd.	1966	1:1.5	74	P
Heavy Engineering Corporation	1956	1:1.2	170	L
Jessop & Co. Ltd.	1958	1:0.05	211	L
Mining & Allied Machinery Corp. Ltd.	1965	1:0.1	240	L
Triveni Structurals	1965	1:0.8	156	L
Bharat Pumps & Compressors Ltd.	1970	1:1.8	87	L
Biecco Lawrie Ltd.	1919	1:0.3	627	L
Central Electronics Ltd.	1974	1:0.9	74	L
National Instruments Ltd.	1957	1:4.8	667	L
Central Inland Water Transport Corp. Ltd.	1964	1:2.1	353	L
Garden Reach Shipbuilders & Engineers Ltd.	1967	1:0.7	123	L
Scooters India Ltd.	1972	1:5.5	604	L
Bharat Opthalmic Glass Ltd.	1972	1:1.8	259	L

(continued overleaf)

APPENDIX 1 (continued)

ENTERPRISES WITH LARGE ACCUMULATED DEFICITS (1981–82) (INDIA)

Enterprise (1)	Date of incorporation (2)	Equity– loan ratio (3)	Deficit as % of equity (4)	Profit/Loss during the year (5)
Mandya National Paper Mills Ltd.	1957	1:1.1	69	L
Rehabilitation Industries Corp. Ltd.	1959	1:0	627	L
Tannery & Footwear Corp. of India Ltd.	1969	1:1.8	222	L
Banana & Fruit Development Corp. Ltd.	1964	1:1.3	269	L
National Textile Corp. Ltd. (A.P. etc.)	1974	1:1.9	84	L
NTC (Delhi etc.) Ltd.	1974	1:1.3	173	L
NTC (Maharashtra North) Ltd.	1974	1:1.7	116	L
NTC (Maharashtra South) Ltd.	1974	1:1.7	120	L
NTC (UP) Ltd.	1974	1:2.0	228	L
NTC (W. Bengal etc.) Ltd.	1974	1:2.1	242	L
Elgin Mills Ltd.	1864	1:2.6	317	L
Cotton Corp. of India Ltd.	1970	1:0.01	269	P
Jute Corp. of India Ltd.	1971	1:7.5	1297	L
Tea Trading Corp. of India Ltd.	1971	1:0.6	54	L
Hindustan Prefab. Ltd.	1953	1:0.02	129	P
Hindustan Steel Works Construction Ltd.	1964	1:1.7	251	L
Engineering Projects (I) Ltd.	1970	1:12.7	719	L
National Industrial Corp. Ltd.	1954	1:1.9	95	P
National Small Industries Corp. Ltd.	1955	1:2.6	67	L

Source: Bureau of Public Enterprises, *Public Enterprises Survey 1981–82*, Vol. 3 (New Delhi, 1983).

APPENDIX 2

ENTERPRISES WITH LARGE ACCUMULATED DEFICITS (1980–81) (PAKISTAN)

Enterprise (1)	Date of incorporation (2)	Equity–loan ratio (3)	Deficit as % of equity (4)	Profit/Loss during the year (5)
Antibiotics Pr. Ltd.	1973	1:1.9	363	L
Ittehad Pesticides	1973	1:3.3	58	L
Kurram Chemical Co. Ltd.	1973	1:5.6	196	L
Pakdyes & Chemicals Ltd.	1973	1:0.2	134	P (very small)
Pakistan PVC Ltd.	1973	1:4.3	360	L
Ravi Rayon Ltd.	1973	1:2.1	100	P
Ravi Engineering	1973	1:9.5	495	P
Swat Ceramics Co. Ltd.	1973	1:2.6	91	P (very small)
Swat Elutriation Plan	1973	1:1.3	74	P (very small)
National Fertiliser Marketing Ltd.	1973	1:0.	472	L
Bannu Sugar Mills		1:0.4	1067	L
Utility Stores Corp.	1971	1:6.3	167	L
Printing Corp. of Pakistan	1968	1:2.9	264	L

Source: *Government Sponsored Corporations*, 1980–81 (Islamabad, 1982).

APPENDIX 3–A

EQUITY–LOAN RATIOS OF PUBLIC ENTERPRISES IN PAKISTAN – BY SECTOR
(1980–81)

Sector	Equity–loan ratio (1: –)						
	All equity	0–0.5	0.5–1.0	1.0–2.0	2.0–3.0	3.0 & above	Total
(1)	(2)	(3)	(4)	(5)	(6)	(7)	(8)
Banking	5	1				1	7
Financial	2		1		1	3	7
Insurance	1	1	1				3
Industry	2	3	2	6	6	11	30
Oil and gas		3	2		2	3	10
Transport & communications	1	2				2	5
Public service	1	1	1		1	3	7
Printing & publication	1		1		1		3
Mining						2	2
Trade and commerce	1	1	1				3
Engineering and consultancy	2					2	4
	16	12	9	6	11	27	81

Source: *Government Sponsored Corporations 1980–81* (Islamabad, 1982).

APPENDIX 3–B

EQUITY–LOAN RATIO BY SIZE OF PAID-UP CAPITAL (ORDINARY) (1980–81)
(PAKISTAN)

Size of paid-up capital (ordinary) (Mill. Rs.)	Equity–loan ratio (1: –)						
	All equity	0–0.5	0.5–1.0	1.0–2.0	2.0–3.0	3.0 and above	Total
(1)	(2)	(3)	(4)	(5)	(6)	(7)	(8)
A (Below 10)	1	2		1	3	9	16
B 10–25	5	2	2	2	1	4	16
C 25–50	4	1	2	1	1	4	13
D 50–100	5	3	2		2	1	13
E 100 and above	1	4	2	2	2	9	20
	16	12	8	6	9	27	78

Source: *Government Sponsored Corporations 1980–81* (Islamabad, 1982).

APPENDIX 3–C

EQUITY–LOAN RATIO BY NET PROFIT (LOSS) RESULTS (1980–81)

(PAKISTAN)

Net profit as % of paid-up capital	Equity–loan ratio (1: –)						
	All equity	0–0.5	0.5–1.0	1.0–2.0	2.0–3.0	3.0 and above	Total
(1)	(2)	(3)	(4)	(5)	(6)	(7)	(8)
Loss	2	3	1	1	2	7	16
0–10	4	2	1	1	3	2	13
10–25	2	2	1		1	3	19
25–50	1	3	1	2	1	3	11
50–100	2	1	1		4	8	16
100–200	2			2		1	5
200 and above	4	2	2			1	9
	17	13	7	6	11	25	79

Source: *Government Sponsored Corporations 1980–81* (Islamabad, 1982).

APPENDIX 3–D

EQUITY–LOAN RATIO BY AGE OF ENTERPRISE (1980–81)

(PAKISTAN)

Date of incorporation	Equity–loan ratio (1: –)						
	All equity	0–0.5	0.5–1.0	1.0–2.0	2.0–3.0	3.0 and above	Total
(1)	(2)	(3)	(4)	(5)	(6)	(7)	(8)
Before 1960	2	3			1	5	11
1960–65	1	1					2
1965–70		1			1	1	3
1970–75	12	5	9	6	7	18	57
1975–80		1			1	3	5
1980 and later	1	1				1	3
	16	12	9	6	10	28	81

Source: *Government Sponsored Corporations 1980–81* (Islamabad, 1982).

APPENDIX 3–E

FINANCIAL EXPENSES AND EQUITY–LOAN RATIO (1981–82)

(PAKISTAN)

Financial expenses as per cent of total expenses	Equity–loan ratio (1: –)						
	All equity	0–0.5	0.5–1.0	1.0–2.0	2.0–3.0	3.0 and above	Total
(1)	(2)	(3)	(4)	(5)	(6)	(7)	(8)
Below 5	1		1		2	2	6
5–10	1	3		2	1		7
10–15				1		2	3
15–20				1		3	4
20–25				1		2	3
25–30	1				1	1	3
30 and above					1		1
	3	3	1	5	5	10	27

Source: Experts Advisory Cell (Pakistan).

APPENDIX 4–A

EQUITY–LOAN RATIO BY SECTOR (1981–82)

(INDIA)

Sector	Equity–loan ratio (1: –)						
	All equity	0–0.5	0.5–1.0	1.00–2.00	2.00–3.00	3.00 & above	Total
(1)	(2)	(3)	(4)	(5)	(6)	(7)	(8)
1. Enterprise under construction	3	1	2	2		1	9
2. Steel	1		1	4			6
3. Minerals and metals		5	4	3		1	13
4. Coal				1	2	2	5
5. Petroleum	3	3		1	3	2	12
6. Chemicals and pharmaceuticals	2	3	7	4	4	1	21
7. Heavy chemicals	1	4	2	5	1	1	14
8. Medium and light engineering	1	2	6	7	2	1	19
9. Transportation equipment		3	2	2	2	2	11
10. Consumer goods	3		4	4	1		12

(continued on next page)

APPENDIX 4–A (continued)

Sector (1)	*Equity–loan ratio (1: –)*						
	All equity (2)	0–0.5 (3)	0.5–1.0 (4)	1.00–2.00 (5)	2.00–3.00 (6)	3.00 & above (7)	Total (8)
11. Agro-based enterprises	3	5	1	1			10
12. Textiles		1	1	5	5		12
13. Trading & marketing services	6	4	3	2		3	18
14. Transportation services	2		2			5	9
15. Contract and construction services	1	2		1		4	8
16. Industrial devel. & technical consultancy services	5		1	1		1	8
17. Development of small industries					1		1
18. Tourist services		1	1				2
19. Financial services				1		2	3
20. Section 25 companies	1		1			1	3
21. Insurance companies							
22. Others: central govt. owned but not managed	3	1	3	1	2	3	13
	35	35	41	45	23	30	209

Source: *Public Enterprises Survey 1981–82*, Bureau of Public Enterprises (New Delhi, 1983).

APPENDIX 4–B

EQUITY–LOAN RATIO BY SIZE OF PAID-UP CAPITAL (1981–82)

(INDIA)

Size of paid-up capital (Rs)	Equity–loan ratio (1: –)						
	All equity	0–0.5	0.5–1.0	1.0–2.0	2.0–3.0	3.0 & above	Total
(1)	(2)	(3)	(4)	(5)	(6)	(7)	(8)
A	15	3		5		2	25
B	5	1	2	2	1		11
C	10	13	15	15	3	12	68
D	2	5	5	10	10	2	34
E	2	3	6	5	2	2	20
F	1	1	2	1	1	4	10
G		7	9	7	4	3	30
	35	33	39	45	21	25	209

Source: *Public Enterprises Survey 1981–82*, BPE (New Delhi, 1983).

APPENDIX 4–C

EQUITY–LOAN RATIOS BY NET PROFIT (LOSS) RESULTS (1981–82)

(INDIA)

Net profit as % of equity	Equity–loan ratio (1: –)						
	All equity	0–0.5	0.5–1.0	1.0–2.00	2.0–3.0	3.0 & above	Total
(1)	(2)	(3)	(4)	(5)	(6)	(7)	(8)
Loss	9	19	15	22	9	9	83
0–10	1	5	9	8	2	2	27
10–25	4	7	10	3	3	6	33
25–50	4	1	4	3	5	5	22
50–100	5	1		4	3	4	17
100–200	5		1		1		7
200 and above	5			2	1	2	10
	33	33	39	42	24	28	199

Source: *Public Enterprises Survey 1981–82*, BPE (New Delhi, 1983).

APPENDIX 4–CI

EQUITY–LOAN RATIOS AND GROSS PROFIT RATES (1981–82)

(INDIA)

Gross profit as % of capital employed	Equity–loan ratio (1: –)						
	0	0–0.5	0.5–1.0	1.0–2.0	2.0–3.0	3.0 & above	Total
(1)	(2)	(3)	(4)	(5)	(6)	(7)	(8)
Below 0	8	12	12	19	8	8	67
0–10	2	7	5	10	4	7	35
10–20	3	7	14	5	6	7	42
20–30	2	5	4	5	3	2	21
30–50	9	1		2	2	1	15
50–75	4						4
75–100							
100 and above	1		1	1			3
	29	32	36	42	23	25	187

Source: *Public Enterprises Survey 1981–82*, BPE (New Delhi, 1983).

APPENDIX 4–D

EQUITY–LOAN RATIOS BY AGE OF ENTERPRISE (1981–82)

(INDIA)

Date of incorporation	Equity–loan ratio (1: –)						
	All equity	0–0.5	0.5–1.0	1.0–2.0	2.0–3.0	3.0 & above	Total
(1)	(2)	(3)	(4)	(5)	(6)	(7)	(8)
Before 1960	3	9	8	7	7	5	39
1960–65	2	1	7	7	4	4	25
1965–70		3	7	4	2	1	17
1970–75	2	8	9	11	5	8	43
1975–80	14	8	4	13	2	5	46
1980 and later	6	3	3	2	1	1	16
	27	32	38	44	21	24	186

Source: *Public Enterprises Survey 1981–82*, BPE (New Delhi, 1983).

SPE–K

APPENDIX 5
CAPITAL STRUCTURES AND NET RETURNS
(IN RUPEES)

	Enterprise A	Enterprise B	Enterprise C	Enterprise D
An example of high returns				
1. Equity capital	100	20	200	20
2. Reserves	100	100	–	–
3. Loans	20	100	20	200
4. Total investment	220	220	220	220
5. Return (before interest)	44	44	44	44
6. Interest on loans at 10%	2	10	2	20
7. Net return after interest (5 minus 6)	42	34	42	24
8. Net return as % of equity capital (7 as % of 1)	42	170	21	120
9. Net return as % of shareholders' equity (7 as % of 1 + 2)	21	28.3	21	120
10. Return as % of total investment (5 as % of 4)	20	20	20	20
An example of low returns				
11. Return (before interest)	17.6	17.6	17.6	17.6
12. Interest on loans	2	10	2	20
13. Net return after interest (11 minus 12)	15.6	7.6	15.6	−2.4
14. Net return as % of equity capital (13 as % of 1)	15.6	38	7.8	−12
15. Net return as % of shareholders' equity (13 as % of 1 + 2)	7.8	6.3	7.8	−12
16. Return as % of total investment	8	8	8	8

APPENDIX 6A
RESERVES AND PROFIT RETENTION (1980–81)
(PAKISTAN)

Reserves as % of paid up capital (ordinary)	Dividend as % of net profit							Total
	0	0–10	10–25	25–50	50–75	75–100	100 and above	
(1)	(2)	(3)	(4)	(5)	(6)	(7)	(8)	(9)
Negative	7							7
0–10	4		1	1				6
10–25	3		1		2	1	1	8
25–50	5			1				6
50–75	2			2				4
75–100	2	1		1		1		5
100–200	2		5	4				11
200 and above	6	6	3	2				17
	31	7	10	11	2	2	1	64

Source: Government Sponsored Corporations 1980–81 (Islamabad, 1982)

APPENDIX 6B
RESERVES AND PROFIT RETENTION (1981–82)
(INDIA)

Reserves as % of paid up capital	Dividend as % of net profit							Total
	0	0–10	10–25	25–50	50–75	75–100	100 and above	
(1)	(2)	(3)	(4)	(5)	(6)	(7)	(8)	(9)
Negative	21		1	1	1			24
0–10	8							8
10–25	7			2		1		10
25–50	2	1	2	2	1			8
50–75	5				1			6
75–100	2	1	1	3	1			8
100–200	7	3	3	3	4			20
200 and above	3	9	13	5	1			31
	55	14	20	16	8	2	—	115

Source: Public Enterprise Survey 1981–82, B.P.E. (New Delhi, 1983)

APPENDIX 7A
RESERVES AND DIVIDEND RATES (1980–81)
(PAKISTAN)

Reserves as % of paid-up capital (ordinary)	Dividend rate %				
	Below 5	5–10	10–15	15 and above	Total
(1)	(2)	(3)	(4)	(5)	(6)
Negative					
0–10	1			1	2
10–25	1	1	1	1	4
25–50				2	2
50–75				2	2
75–100			2	1	3
100–200		1	5	3	9
200 and above				8	8
	2	2	8	18	30

Source: Government Sponsored Corporations 1980–81 (Islamabad, 1982)

APPENDIX 7B
RESERVES AND DIVIDEND RATES (1980–81)
(INDIA)

Reserves as % of paid-up capital	Dividend rate %				
	Below 5	5–10	10–15	15 and above	Total
(1)	(2)	(3)	(4)	(5)	(6)
Negative	1	1	1	1	4
0–10			1		1
10–25	2	2			4
25–50	2	3	1		6
50–75	1	1		1	3
75–100		3	3		6
100–200		4	3	2	9
200 and above		4	9	14	27
	6	18	18	18	60

Source: Public Enterprise Survey 19871–82, B.P.E. (New Delhi, 1983)

PART THREE

Public Enterprise and the Public Exchequer

INTRODUCTION

The relationship between public enterprise and the public exchequer is a topic which has special relevance to developing economies. The financial results and strategies of public enterprises have often been treated as matters of management efficiency. There is no need to de-emphasise this view; in fact in the less developed countries there is particular merit in such an approach. However, the thought that is projected here is that too little recognition is given, *in effective terms*, to the implications of the financial results and strategies of public enterprises for the public exchequer. The impacts are both quantitative and qualitative. (Part II already contains some references to these aspects.) Several aspects of public enterprise operations overlap those of the public exchequer and the budgeting authority. It is, therefore, desirable to conceive of mutual compatibility in operational terms. This is not a plea for eclipsing the managerial autonomy of public enterprises.

In the course of this study we shall concentrate on three aspects, using Indian data in building up the argument and for illustration: the implications of pricing, the impacts on the tax strategies, and capital losses. Several issues of detail are kept aside – e.g., allocational or investment implications of pricing.

1

Pricing

Let us consider pricing first. Prices appear to be a matter for managerial determination, subject to any constraints that exist at the hands of public agencies for price control. The idea implicit in this notion is that prices essentially rest on costs. If an enterprise fixes prices far divorced from the cost basis, another enterprise can snatch away the customers, assuming that competition exists. Where it does not, prices can far exceed costs; yet from the consumer's point of view special reason has to be produced before a non-cost-based price is demanded of him. Enterprises raising high profits, because of monopoly power in ultimate analysis, tend to implement, in effect, prices that have no basis in costs but contain elements of taxation. A public enterprise can do it with greater ease than a private monopoly, the more surely when it is not exposed to control by any monopoly commission.

Herein lies one version of the overlap between public enterprise and the public exchequer. The former, through internal managerial decision, extracts from a group of citizens, its customers, incomes that strictly can only be demanded by a taxing authority.

Two problems arise. First, the criteria of levying a tax are not necessarily the same as those underlying a high price. The latter is a function of the inelasticity of demand in a given market. There can be no presumption that the customers touched are those that satisfy the criteria applicable to potential tax bearers. Take, for example, residential consumers of electricity. Where these happen to be chosen for high prices, can we at once be certain that they are the ones that the government would have singled out for taxation?

Second, tax measures receive parliamentary attention. They are discussed and voted by Parliament; by implication, their "relative" justification in the income-raising strategy of the government is established through specific debate. Besides, the decision represents a socio-economic preference that has the stamp of governmental and legislative sanction. On the other hand, high-profit making prices are willed by managers, whose status does not justify their assumption of the governmental and legislative prerogatives implicit in the decision. Herein lies a constitutional impropriety.

There is another interesting aspect of the overlap. Assume that the profits arising from high prices are really intended by the government as a convenient means of raising revenues for the public exchequer. Now the criticism that the managers are, *questionably*, assuming tax powers, might be weakened. But the point remains that the Finance Minister is informally using a public enterprise for indirect tax measures and, whether by intent or otherwise, escapes liability to parliamentary scrutiny of the ethics and the economics of the measure. In this way public enterprise becomes a vehicle for the minister escaping parliamentary accountability.

Where the high profits do not reach the government through dividends or as a share in profits, public enterprise effectively monopolises the power to decide on the use of the resources extracted from citizens, over and above the due costs of their intake as customers. The profits may go into expansions, at one end, or into "conspicuous consumption" through enhanced employee benefits at another. In either case the canons of determination that ought to involve the custodians of the public exchequer, do not bring them into the decisional picture.

So far the argument was presented in terms of profits. In the opposite case of losses, public enterprises entail elements of subsidy. Once again, it is far from certain that the group of citizens, that constitute the customers of losing enterprises, are the ones that the budget process ending in Parliamentary approval may have identified, as those that deserve soft treatment. All the comments made in the preceding paragraphs apply here too.

A simple illustration of the point may be drawn from the results of the State Electricity Boards. The return on capital (after meeting operating and maintenance charges and depreciation and excluding the electricity duties) compared with the Venkataraman Committee's target of 11 per cent in 1981, as follows, as per available data.[1]

Above 11 per cent   Kerala, Karnataka and Tamilnadu

9–11 per cent   Orissa, Gujarat, West Bengal, Uttar

	Pradesh, Punjab, Maharashtra and Andhra Pradesh
1–9 per cent	Madhya Pradesh, Rajasthan, Bihar and Haryana
Below 0 per cent	Himachal Pradesh

An interesting point lent by these data is that in some regions electricity consumers derive subsidised prices – extremely highly in a few cases; whereas in some others they do not. It is doubtful if these diversities received due sanction from the public exchequer level and if, in all-India parlance, they reflect justified equity.

There is an asymmetry between the situation of high profits and that of losses. The former, along with their tax implications, prevail in the case of a private monopoly as well, though public policies of monopoly control seek to restrict them either through price or profit constraints or through the promotion of competition. Situations of subsidy through losses are, over the long run, characteristic predominantly of public enterprises, on the assumption that they can survive despite losses, whereas private enterprises go out of existence in no time. Losing enterprises thus present a unique aspect of the integral relationship between public enterprise and the public exchequer.

The significance of the above analysis can be illustrated with reference to the net revenues derived by Indian public enterprises. The data contained in the Public Enterprises Survey of the Bureau of Public Enterprises (BPE) are selectively picked up – in respect of enterprises whose gross profits exceeded 30 per cent (or whose losses exceeded 20 per cent) of the capital employed. (Gross profit represents net revenue before interest and tax; and capital employed represents net block plus working capital.) Appendix 1–A processes the data so as to establish how variously individual enterprises of the profit-making category earned in excess of a 10 per cent norm. The norm is a matter of judgement representing the cost of capital or admissible return on capital, inclusive of self-financing customary in the corporate sector. The last column expresses the excesses as percentages of gross revenues. These may be considered as a blunt measure of the elements of indirect taxation contained in the prices. These, surely, do not represent accurate magnitudes.[2] They are illustrative of the principle enunciated here. As one may appreciate, they are bound to be different if one assumes a different norm than 10 per cent. There is room for such a different assumption especially on the score of the self-financing element of the norm. The higher this is, the lower the excesses of actual net profits over the norm tend to be; hence the lower the tax elements appear to be.

Appendix 1–B seeks to indicate the diverse amounts of shortfall below the 10 per cent norm in the case of the heavily losing enterprises. These may be considered as a blunt measure of the elements of subsidy contained in the prices. Here it may be noted that, with an assumption of a higher norm than 10 per cent, the short-falls tend to be larger than those estimated in the last column; correspondingly the elements of subsidy imputable to the prices also tend to be higher.

It is now easy to notice how elements of public exchequer policy are enmeshed in public enterprise finances, escaping Parliamentary scrutiny and well-deliberated justification, case by case.[3] Not that no justification exists in any of the cases, e.g. the high prices on oil; but several cases are question-begging – especially in the category of losing enterprises, and about relativities on the whole.

A brief comment may be made, further, on the findings emerging from the "illustrative" figure work of Appendix 1 (A and B). As between the tax and the subsidy elements the latter magnitudes are larger, on the whole. In other words, heavy subsidies manifest themselves through public enterprises, without due parliamentary process. Apart from this, the Appendix does not cover the less-than-30 per cent gross profit cases; and there can be no certainty as to whether the excesses over the norm in their cases work out high or low in relation to the respective "turnover" figures.

Reverting to the main argument, we can take the view that some degree of involvement of the public exchequer in public enterprise finances can be deemed to be in existence when the government adopts the strategy of determining financial targets for public enterprises. For, as envisaged in the UK:

> When the (financial) target has been settled for the industry, the Secretary of State will announce it to Parliament. He will indicate the main assumptions on which it is based: for example, any particular social or sectoral objectives which the Government has set the industry, and which may have

affected the level of the target, the broad complications for the pricing policy; and any other important factors of which Parliament and the public should know when they subsequently judge the industry's performance against the target.[4]

This represents an exceptional circumstance in the history of public enterprise on a global scale. There are very few instances of financial targetting, outside the UK. The technique of "contrat de programme" adopted by France calls for mention. This determines the financial relationships between the public enterprise and the public exchequer.[5] However, it does not cover the entire bulk of public enterprises. There is provision in the Kenyan Acts – e.g. those governing the railways and the ports – for governmental fixation of financial targets; but this has not been implemented. Financial targets for public enterprises, in the spirit of the UK White Paper, do not exist in India. Even where the Act contemplates them – e.g. in the case of the Electricity Boards[6] – "until now, however, no State Government has specified any such surplus."[7]

Let us turn to a few subtle aspects of the budgetary implications of public enterprise profits or losses. Are they absent in the case of a public enterprise that breaks even? Not necessarily. Though there is neither a profit nor a loss, there may have been cross-subsidisations among consumer groups, not for commercial reasons traceable to conditions of joint costs, but for other reasons. These may border on assumptions of equity and involve either differential prices – i.e. prices which are not cost-related – or uniform prices[8] under conditions of unequal costs. How far such revenue strategies of enterprises agree with public preferences should be a matter of concern for the government, at the level of the public exchequer. Both the price level and the major characteristics of the price structure adopted by a public enterprise are matters that ought to attract the interest of public agencies supervising public enterprises, under the guidelines emerging from the Treasury.

2

Tax Impacts

It has been quite common for critics to look at the finances of public enterprises and be content with treating them as a reflection of their efficiency or otherwise. Occasionally these have been used as an argument in support of public enterprise or against it. But the kind of implications they have for the public exchequer has not received the wide appreciation that it merits. Let us start with the tax impacts.

An investment in a public enterprise ordinarily is supported by a public borrowing, the more so when (i) budget surpluses are exceptional and (ii) the magnitude of investments is large. Both these circumstances are relevant to India as well as many other developing countries. The minimum obligation on the part of public enterprise finances is to provide the public exchequer with enough incomes to service the public debt concerned. Or else, any shortfall has to be met through tax measures, unless it is decided to meet it through deficit financing or borrowings.

An interesting question arises at this point. Is every public investment designed to earn not less than is sufficient to cover all costs, including capital costs? The answer calls for definitional precision on public enterprise. It may be understood "to be an activity in which the majority ownership and/or control is non-private and which is intended to be viable through sales activity on the basis of price–cost relationships."[9] Hospitals, zoos, and parks do not satisfy this concept, but all the enterprises covered by BPE should. (Incidentally, the viability criterion is valid, independently of the reality of initial gestation and occasional business fluctuations. In both situations appropriate accounting techniques are available. A word on the qualification of social returns will come later on.)

Do public enterprises have a record of contributing to the public exchequer the interest charges on the public debt for which they are responsible? There is no uniform answer on a global scale. But there is enough cause for disquiet on the following grounds:

(a)   The loan component of the investment is, in some cases, free of interest; in others it carries a rather low rate of interest; in yet others there is a moratorium on interest payments; and in several cases the interest is shown as accrued but is not actually paid by the enterprises to the government.

(b)   Interest payments in some cases are fictitious in the sense that like amounts (or larger sums) are simultaneously received as deficit grants by the enterprises from the public exchequer.

(c)   As regards the equity segment of the public investments a large number of enterprises have not paid any returns to the public exchequer – in India as well as elsewhere (e.g. Pakistan and Kenya) – out of inability in a majority of cases and out of un-willingness to declare dividends in several cases.

It would be interesting to present, at this stage, actual material illustrative of the public enterprise–public exchequer relationship in India in so far as the "current flows" (of a revenue character, not capital transactions) are concerned. The magnitudes of the relevant figures for 1980–81 and 1981–82 are given in the following table.

	1980–81 (Rs. crores)	1981–82 (Rs. crores)
1. Capital employed[10]	18,207	21,865
2. Central government's Investments[11] (equity plus loan)	17,013	19,666
3. Interest receipts[12]	1,399	1,601
4. Dividend receipts[13]	8	11
5. Total (3) plus (4)	1,407	1,612
6. Approximate interest cost of related public debt[14] (1) × 6.4%; (2) × 6.7%	1,165	1,465

In sheer terms of arithmetic, public enterprises as a whole (covered by BPE Survey) did return to the Central government slightly more than the bare interest costs of the public debt concerned during 1981–83. One cannot be sanguine about this, however, for several serious reasons.

The first stems from our initial observation that meeting the government's interest costs of public debt is a *minimal* responsibility of public enterprises (which itself may not have been fulfilled in several earlier years). We should not forget that governments have budget strategies on the composition of revenues – broadly as between tax and non-tax receipts. As the needs of current expenditures expand, and those of developmental expenditures as well, it would be a fruitful strategy to raise resources "equitably" under both categories. Or else, as the non-tax receipts of which incomes from public enterprises are a part, remain static or expand rather nominally, the burdens of tax effort are likely to expand. In a revenue structure[15] with taxes on commodities and services constituting 58 per cent of the total or about three-quarters of all tax revenues or more than thrice the revenues from direct taxes, it is possible that additional tax efforts tend to be regressive. In one sense this is to be considered as a macro consequence of public enterprise operations.

The argument gains in substance from two facts. First, as revealed in the Mid-Term Appraisal (Sixth Five Year Plan, 1980–83),[16] deficit financing and uncovered gap has been growing: e.g. from 1.46 per cent of GDP (at current prices) in 1977–78 to 2.39 per cent in 1980–83. In terms of gross domestic savings (at current prices), it grew from 6.42 per cent to 9.92 per cent. The needs of the public exchequer for increased current inflows are incontrovertible.

Second, public enterprises occupy a dominant position in the capital expenditure strategy of the government and, by implication, in the public debt structure. For instance, more than four-fifths of the developmental capital expenditures of the central government during 1982–83 were on commercial and industrial activities.[17] Besides, a sizeable part of the country's investments in such activities takes place through the public sector. For instance, no less than 50 per cent of investments under the Plans have been in the public sector.

Putting these facts together, we can infer that the revenue base for the public exchequer has been progressively sucked into the public sector. Government revenues, therefore, increasingly have to look to public enterprise contributions and negate the force of the Planning Commission's observation[18] that:

> at present a number of Central enterprises are either incurring losses or are not yielding adequate return on the investments made.

To express the idea in another way, the investments in public enterprises represent corresponding diversions from the private sector. They have an opportunity cost. That they should earn commensurately with it would be not only in the immediate interest of the public exchequer but also in conformity with the distributional implications that ought to be implicit in the concept of public enterprise. This idea may be explained in the following terms. A surplus is expected to accrue at the public levels, instead of profits going to private investors. Where this does not materialise it would really be in the ultimate interest of the public exchequer itself to rethink on the comparative advantage that individual public enterprises possess, so that they will exist only where comparative advantage exists or comparative advantage is enriched by fair means.

Let us discuss another aspect of public enterprise contributions to the public exchequer as investor. This investor, unlike investors in general, has not exerted itself in the direction of high dividend incomes. This is true not only of India but of several developing countries. The Indian data suggest that during 1981–82, 106 enterprises made net profits, but only 54 declared dividends. Only about six per cent of the aggregate net profit reached the public exchequer as a current flow of income. (For details see Appendix 2.) Of the top ten profit-making enterprises only six declared dividends, three of them using less than five per cent of their net profits for the purpose.

There are at least three reasons why the situation calls for comment. First, the budgeting position of the government being far from comfortable, higher incomes from public enterprises than are coming in are desirable. Or else, the public exchequer may be constrained to resort to measures of eventual inequity through taxation and deficit financing. Second, emphasis on higher dividend incomes will prompt government directors on the boards of

public enterprises to exert themselves in the direction of effica-
cious monitoring of enterprise operations. Third, decisions concerning the use of net revenues – in some cases very high for
reasons of public policy – e.g., oil and state trading, will rightly
shift to the government level if they substantially move into the
public exchequer in the first place. (They may move back, but on
government decision.) The resources will be available for any
channel of public expenditure that the budgeting authority and
processes favour.

   We shall turn next to a rigorous analysis of the very concept of
overall net earnings of all public enterprises. In one sense it is
meaningful. The budgeting authority has a practical interest in
ensuring that, without special reason, government investments in
enterprises do not contribute to a budgetary deficit, or more
positively, perhaps, that they contribute a desired net quantum of
revenue. Apart from this, real significance should attach to the
composition of the figure. From several points of view, it is the
individual net revenue results that merit critical notice. Apart
from their purport for efficiency scrutinies of individual enterprises, these have relevance to the public exchequer itself, though
this has not been adequately recognised yet. As already suggested,
diverse net revenues imply diverse tax or subsidy elements in
different prices, entailing income transfers among citizen groups
without Parliamentary sanction. Besides, the notion that some
deficits are offset by some profits is far less commendable than the
aim of maximising the prospective revenue contributions from
every enterprise, unless established reasons of social policy stand
in the way.

   That this issue warrants attention in India may be illustrated by
the extremely heterogeneous net revenue structure of public enterprises. Sector by sector, some enterprises made profits, while
some others made losses, as indicated in Appendix 3. On the whole
net profits accrued on a total of Rs 79.68 crores of equity capital
employed, whereas losses characterised Rs 46.42 crores of equity
(in 1981–82). To minimise the budgetary impacts of the latter
should be a major aim of public exchequer policy, independently
of complacency on the overall position.[19] The losing enterprises
must have brought in a double disadvantage to the public exchequer. First, through non-payment of dividend incomes they
must have compelled taxation to fill the gap. As a rough estimate

the interest costs of public debt corresponding to the equity capital of the enterprises concerned may have been about Rs 325 crores; this must have been the gap that taxation had to aim at filling (whether it did, it is difficult to establish). Second, by probably necessitating public sector grants (even if termed euphemistically as "advances" to feed the losses), they must have, again, aggravated the needs of tax effort or public borrowings. At the minimum the chances of any tax reliefs were weakened.

3

Capital Losses

We turn, finally, to the question of capital losses suffered by public enterprises. These have occurred in many countries – e.g. India, Pakistan,[20] Kenya[21] and the UK.[22] We do not go into the reasons for capital losses; our interest at this point is to address the policy strategy on the part of the public exchequer.

How wide and serious the problem is, in India, can be seen from the figures of accumulated deficits of certain enterprises tabulated in Appendix 1 of Part 2. The aggregate capital lost in enterprises whose deficits exceed the equity is no less than Rs 13,78 crores. This works out at about 12% of all equity capital, excluding enterprises "under construction."

This is a disquieting figure, but it represents a fact of life; and public exchequer policies should promptly be geared to deal with them. There is no choice.

Of course, one has to explore if any of these accumulated deficits are likely to be wiped out in the near future by profits. While this line can never be ignored, it is time that we were realistic in policy measures. It will be helpful in every way to recognise the more-or-less permanent losses of capital, whatever the reasons – some are in fact in the nature of costs of national gestation in development – and formulate schemes of capital write-off. That would be neither wrong nor unprecedented. (In the UK – even an advanced country could experience a capital loss in public enterprise – capital write-offs were implemented in respect of British Steel Corporation and British Railways Board on more than one occasion.)

Not to decide on such a step amounts to perpetuating the fiction that there exists so-and-so capital outlay while in fact it is not there in terms of assets or earning power. Even on grounds of ideology, a bold measure of write off is preferable to inaction, in that it will thence forward save the public enterprise sector from continuous ridicule for losses and equally materially relieve the hard-working

CAPITAL LOSSES   169

managers from undeserved stigma of incompetence on grounds of
losses that signify the impacts of lost capital.

However, it has to be noted that the burdens of the public
exchequer in respect of the related public debt will continue. The
point is that these would be no less if the write-off were not
undertaken. But the write-off helps keep the record straight and
immensely improves the interface between public enterprise and
the public exchequer, between the managers and Parliament, and
between the consumers and the enterprises.

Losses of capital are an unfortunate fact of public enterprise
history in many countries. To admit these may be a delicate
political problem. But not to do so would amount to perpetuating a
fiction of public investment in the records of the public exchequer.

4

Conclusion

The above analysis and argument have been in terms of the central government's public enterprises. (Even here the BPE data we used did not cover several major public enterprises like railways, posts and telegraphs, port trusts and banks.) There are many enterprises at the state government level. It has not been possible to introduce data on them on the same scale as those for the BPE enterprises. However, the broad conclusion that their performance has been discouraging, on the whole, seems to be valid. For instance the Chairman of the Eighth Finance Commission recently "expressed concern at the continued losses in state undertakings."[23] The Planning Minister observed as recently as in December 1983,

> In spite of the efforts at additional resources, the State Electricity Boards, some public sector undertakings, and road transport continued to be in the red. The revenue surplus expected from the states had not materialised. Unless the States improved the working of their public undertakings, the prospects of the Seventh Plan would be put into question.[24]

Some specific evidence may be drawn from Andhra Pradesh. The investment of the State government in 1981–82, in equity form, was Rs 304 crores and the return in the form of dividend was Rs 0,5 crores. This worked out at 0.16 per cent on capital, as compared to the government's cost of borrowings at about 5.45 per cent.

Lest it be thought that, though the dividend paid to the government was little, the enterprises may have retained high profits, detailed data are tabulated in Appendix 4. The impression clearly emerges that the overall position was one of losses before tax (at 11.2 per cent on equity). Losses characterised both the co-operative sector and the corporate sector and most sub-categories under each.[25]

These data should suggest that there were budgetary impacts through extra taxation or through impediments to tax reliefs.

As we conclude, let us say a word on social returns, to which reference was made at the very outset. Public enterprises are expected to produce social returns, unlike, or far more deliberately than, private enterprises. In so doing they may experience diminutions in financial returns. Since these are a product of governmental choice, it would be logical that these should be considered as acceptable impacts on the public exchequer.

True, in theory; and in practice *provided* –

(a) that the identified and pre-planned social returns are realised;
(b) that their impacts on the public exchequer are the minimum necessary;
(c) that realising them through given public enterprises represents the most economical and efficient option among the strategies open to the national economy; and
(d) that there is transparency as to the relative roles of the managers and the Treasury in the strategy and as to the impacts on enterprise consumer groups.

All this may sound like a Pandora's box. But there it is. Short of sorting it out, the nation may end up with the fact of adversity for the public exchequer as against the fiction of social returns. Who knows, the latter might, even partially, be a proxy for gains that are not really "social." Our attempt should be a conscious maximisation of the real social returns while minimising the budget adversity, or, to put it in the other way, minimisation of the financial impact on the public exchequer while maximising social returns derivable from public enterprises.

NOTES

1. Central Electricity Authority, *Financial Performance Review* (New Delhi, 1983), p. 9.
2. Besides, I am not raising questions, here, about the economic accuracy of the accounting figures found in the books of public enterprises.
3. For a full discussion, see "Tax and Subsidy Elements in Public Enterprise Prices," *The Review of Economics and Statistics*, Harvard, November 1964, by V.V. Ramanadham.
4. *The Nationalised Industries* (Cmnd. 7131, London 1978), p. 26.
5. Maurice Garner, *Aspects of the French, West German and Swedish experience of*

government relationships with public enterprises, Background Paper 2, National
Economic Development Office (London, 1976), pp. 61–3.

6. Section 59(1), *The Electricity (Supply) Act, 1948.*

7. Central Electricity Authority, *State Electricity Boards: Financial Performance Review*, (New Delhi, 1983), p. 3.

8. For instance, British Telecom observes: "uniform tariffs all over the country are widely seen as fair, despite great variations in the costs of providing the service; and this view cannot be ignored." *Further considerations relating to the British Telecommunications network and proposals to permit competition* (London, 1981), p. 15.

9. V.V. Ramanadham, *The Nature of Public Enterprise* (London, 1984), p. 63.

10. BPE, *Public Enterprises Survey 1981–82*, Vol. 1, p. 6.

11. Ibid., p. 151 and p. 157 (Equity Rs 11,622 crores, Loans Rs 8,044 crores) for 1981–82; p. 154 and p. 159 (1980–81 Vol. 1) – Equity Rs 95.94 crores and Loans Rs 71.19 crores.

12. Ibid., p. 6.

13. Ibid., p. 50.

14. *Report on Currency and Finance 1981–82*, Vol. II, Interest Payments: Rs 2,696 crores and Rs 3,264 crores in 1980–81 and 1981–82 (p. 107), Vol. I: Public Debt Rs 42,162 crores in 1980–81 and Rs 48,084 crores in 1981–82; average rate of interest – 6.4% and 6.7% in 1980–81 and 1981–82.

15. *Report on Currency and Finance 1981–82*, Vol. II, p. 106.

16. Planning Commission, *Sixth Five Year Plan 1980–85*: Mid Term Appraisal (New Delhi, June 1983), Table V.

17. Budget estimates as per Reserve Bank of India, *Report on Currency and Finance 1981–82*, Vol. II, p. 105.

18. *Sixth Five Year Plan 1980–85*, p. 67.

19. A very recent piece of information on losing enterprises comes from a Parliamentary answer that "fifteen public sector units incurred a loss of Rs. 1,000 crores annually," *The Hindu* (10 December 1983).

20. For illustrative information see *Government Sponsored Corporations 1981–82* (Islamabad, 1983).

21. See *Report of the Working Party on Government Expenditures* (Nairobi, 1987).

22. See Annual Reports of British Railways Board and British Steel Corporation.

23. *Economic Times*, 18 May 1983.

24. *Financial Express*, 20 December 1982.

25. These data have all been drawn from *Public Enterprises: A Case for Return on Investment*, prepared on behalf of the Public Enterprise Management Board, Government of Andhra Pradesh, for a Seminar on State Public Enterprises held in November 1983 at Hyderabad.

APPENDIX 1–A

TAX ELEMENTS IN PUBLIC ENTERPRISE PRICES (1981–82)

Enterprise	Capital employed (Rs crores)	Gross profit above 10%	(3) in Rs crores	Turn-over (Rs crores)	(4) as % of (5)
(1)	(2)	(3)	(4)	(5)	(6)
1. Iisco Stanton Pipe & Foundry Co. Ltd.	6.1	42	2.6	17	15.3
2. Ferro Scrap Nigam Ltd.	4.4	22	0.97	4	24.3
3. Cochin Refineries Ltd.	54.6	23	12.6	769	1.6
4. Bharat Petroleum Corp. Ltd.	111.9	23	25.7	1515	1.7
5. Indo-Burma Petroleum Co. Ltd.	11.6	29	3.3	383	0.9
6. Madras Refineries Ltd.	67.6	25	17	733	2.3
7. Oil and National Gas Commission	1536.4	33	507.0	1330	38.1
8. Oil India Ltd.	89.2	211	188.2	314	59.9
9. Lagan Jute Machinery Co. Ltd.	3.6	44	1.6	6	26.7
10. Bharat Earth Movers Ltd.	128.3	20	25.6	222	11.5
11. Hooghly Printing Co.Ltd.	0.2	27	0.05	0.7	0.7
12. Andaman & Nicobar Islands Forest & Plant Dev. Corp. Ltd.	2.6	24	0.63	2	31.5
13. Rajgarh Tea Co. Ltd.	1.3	29	0.38	3	12.7
14. Metal Scrap Trade Corp. Ltd.	2.1	116	2.44	73	3.3
15. Minerals & Metals Trading Corp. of India Ltd.	144.0	33	47.5	1737	2.7
16. State Trading Corporation of India Ltd.	150.7	46	69.3	1867	3.7
17. Air India Charters Ltd.	0.02	140	0.03	3	1.0
18. Indian Railway Construction Co. Ltd.	5.9	32	1.7	25	6.8
19. Engineers India Ltd.	17.1	22	3.8	23	16.5
20. Rail India Technical & Ec. Services Ltd.	9.1	27	2.5	15	16.6

Source for Appendices 1–3: Bureau of Public Enterprises, *Public Enterprises Survey: 1981–82* (New Delhi, 1983).

APPENDIX 1–B

SUBSIDY ELEMENTS IN PUBLIC ENTERPRISE PRICES (1981–82)

Enterprise	Capital employed (Rs crores)	Gross profit above 10%	(3) in Rs crores	Turn-over (Rs crores)	(4) as % of (5)
(1)	(2)	(3)	(4)	(5)	(6)
1. Eastern Coalfields Ltd.	235	39	91.7	346	26.5
2. Braithwaits & Co. Ltd.	14	69	10	16	62.5
3. Mining & Allied Machinery Corp. Ltd.	21	50	10.5	38	27.6
4. Bharat Process & Mechanical Eng. Ltd.	3	65	1.10	4	27.5
5. National Instruments Ltd.	3	51	1.5	4	37.5
6. Hindustan Shipyard Ltd.	22	32	7.0	3	233.3
7. Cycle Corp. of India Ltd.	9	40	3.6	23	15.7
8. National Bicycle Corp. Ltd.	3.5	65	2.3	9	25.6
9. Bharat Opthalmic Glass Ltd.	1.6	51	0.82	0.5	164
10. Tannery & Footwear Corp. of India Ltd.	7	35	2.5	4	67.5
11. Brushware Ltd.	0.05	30	0.01	0.7	1.4
12. Mim Tea Co. Ltd.	0.04	235	0.09	0.3	30.0
13. NTC (Delhi etc.) Ltd.	12	46	5.5	31	17.7
14. NTCP (MP) Ltd.	16	42	6.7	53	12.6
15. NTC (UP) Ltd.	11	69	7.6	34	22.4
16. NTC (W. Bengal etc.)	16	52	8.3	35	23.7
17. Elgin Mills Co. Ltd.	4	110	4.4	26	16.9
18. Bharat Leather Corp.Ltd.	1	49	.49	1	49.0
19. Vayudoot Ltd.	1.3	62	0.80	0.1	800.0
20. Hindustan Steel Works Constn. Ltd.	5	111	5.6	155	3.6

APPENDIX 2

NET PROFITS AND DIVIDENDS (1981–82)

| Sector | Net Profit | | Dividends | | (5) as % of (3) |
| | No. | Rs. lakhs | No. | Rs. lakhs | |
(1)	(2)	(3)	(4)	(5)	(6)
Steel	4	43.48	2	75	1.7
Minerals	8	47.65	2	35	0.7
Coal	2	158.91	-	-	-
Petroleum	11	973.04	10	55.04	5.6
Chemicals	10	159.69	3	9.48	5.9
Heavy Engineering	3	53.05	2	10.44	19.6
Medium and Light Engineering	11	89.41	7	8.40	9.4
Transportation Equipment	5	65.59	4	8.13	12.4
Consumer goods	5	6.98	2	19	2.7
Agro-based Industries	6	2.92	4	19	6.5
Textiles	2	3.50	–	–	–
Trading	12	151.82	90	12.73	8.4
Transportation services	7	57.51	–	–	–
Contract etc.	5	5.31	1	9	1.6
Industrial Development etc.	8	14.50	5	49	3.4
Tourist Services	2	5.11	2	135	26.4
Financial Services	2	28.33	1	110	3.8
Section 25 Cos.	3	15.37	–	–	–
Total:	106	1885.96	54	108.79	5.8

APPENDIX 3

NET PROFITS OR LOSSES AND RELATED EQUITY (1981–82)

Sector	Net profit before tax	Equity capital of profitable enterprises	Net loss before tax	Equity Capital of losing enterprises
	(Rs crores)	(Rs crores)	(Rs crores)	(Rs crores)
(1)	(2)	(3)	(4)	(5)
Steel	43	3222	42	143
Minerals and Metals	47	660	123	618
Coal	159	272	116	1553
Petroleum	973	650	0.4	25
Chemicals and Pharmaceuticals	160	881	227	977
Heavy Engineering	53	192	63	271
Medium and Light Engineering	89	139	10	27
Transportation Equipment	66	164	44	84
Consumer Goods	7	263	10	39
Agro-based Enterprises	3	17	0.2	1
Textiles	4	70	75	324
Trading	152	378	15	16
Transportation Services	58	204	50	2
Contract etc.	5	26	15	40
Industrial Development etc.	20	10	23	6
Tourist Services	5	36	0.5	11
Financial Services	28	152	0.03	5
Section-25 Cos.	15	2	–	–
	18,86	79,68	312	46,42

APPENDIX 4

STATE GOVERNMENT INVESTMENTS IN PUBLIC ENTERPRISES
IN ANDHRA PRADESH (1981–82)

Sector	No. of Enterprises	Equity Investment	Net Profit	Net Profit as % of equity
		(Rs crores)	(Rs crores)	
(1)	(2)	(3)	(4)	(5)
Corporate Sector:				
Development agencies	8	43	3.9	
Production Units	16	63	– 4.2	
Marketing enter- prises	4	5	2.4	
Service organisations	8	95	–29.7	
	36	211	–27.6	–13.1
Co-operative Sector:				
Development agencies	9	75	– 0.5	
Sugar factories	14	12	– 3.5	
Spinning mills	6	6	– 6.3	6.8
	65	304	–33.9	–11.2

Source: Public Enterprise Management Board, Andhra Pradesh (Hyderabad).

PART FOUR

Privatisation in the African Context

INTRODUCTION

The plan of the study may be outlined as follows. The first section deals with the concept of privatisation in its comprehensive coverage. The second brings out the salient features of whatever privatisation has been practised in some African countries. There is a critique of the rationale of privatisation in the third section. And the last one contains an analysis of the problems and implications of the policies of privatisation.

The focus and interest of this presentation is technical. There is no intention to deal with ideological issues.

1

The Concept of Privatisation

Privatisation has been a new trend in several countries and seems to be understood in different ways by different people. Let us, at the outset, delineate the concept in analytical terms in Figure 1.

FIGURE 1

THE CONCEPT OF PRIVATISATION

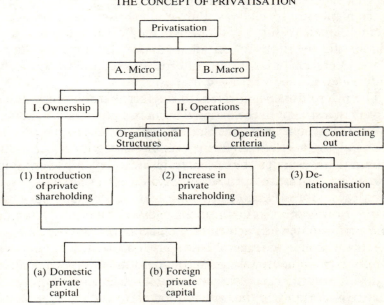

Privatisation at the enterprise level, the clearer aspect of the privatisation concept, can proceed in terms of ownership changes (I) or operational changes (II). The former envisage, on the whole, a reduced public shareholding proportion in one way or another. It comes to the zero level when an enterprise is denationalised (i.e. transferred to the private sector), as is currently contemplated in Kenya in specific cases. In the other cases it is useful to distinguish between domestic capital and foreign capital let into a public enterprise. (The latter might be more zealously welcomed, as in Ethiopia under the 1983 proclamation on joint ventures.)

The concept of operational changes is of significance in a unique sense in the context of developing countries. Ownership changes, especially of the extreme kind – i.e. denationalisation, are not politically easy; yet substantive elements of privatisation can be introduced in the organisational structures and in the operating criteria of the public enterprise as in Sudan (see later paragraphs). Incidentally this angle of privatisation emphasises that the essence of the publicness of the enterprise borders on operational uniqueness rather than on mere ownership.

"Contracting out" has begun to assume importance in developing countries in a special way. Public enterprises are encouraged to promote ancillary units with which they enter into contractual relations for the supply of certain inputs. In this way a certain part of the operations that public enterprises could have themselves undertaken is shed to private units.

The macro dimension refers to the fact that the proportion of private investment in the national economy expands as a sequel to government policies on investment and entrepreneurship. The micro changes cited in the preceding paragraphs themselves culminate in changes at the macro level, unless for every micro change increasing the private proportion of ownership in some cases there are offsetting developments which raise the public share of ownership in other enterprises or bring into being new enterprises under full or majority ownership.

Privatisation in the macro sense is also positive when the government's entrepreneurial decisions on investment imply a relatively high share on the part of private capital – as in Egypt where "the relative importance of the contribution of the public sector in total investment decreased from 90% in the years prior to 1973 to about 76% in 1981–82."[1]

An interesting facet of the privatisation concept may be deduced from a situation in which a joint venture which has substantial public investment may nevertheless "be deemed to belong to the private sector of the economy"[2] – for instance in Egypt. More than semantics is involved here. For, being considered a private sector enterprise entitles it to certain exemptions from the characteristics and obligations attached to public enterprises,[3] and it correspondingly enjoys an enhanced operational autonomy. It comes near the case of AII of figure 1.

To appreciate the comprehensive connotation of privatisation as presented in the preceding paragraphs, is essential in understanding the diverse strands of policy traceable in the rethinking on the size and role of public enterprises in the African context.

2

Privatisation in Some African Countries

This section presents the salient aspects of privatisation measures undertaken in recent years in some African countries – Egypt, Sudan, Ethiopia, and Kenya. The first three represent economies subjected to almost wholesale nationalisations as a matter of socio-economic policy, while Kenya has always been a mixed economy.

A. EGYPT

The Open Door Policy initiated in 1974 encouraged private investment. It is estimated that the contribution of the private sector rose from 10% of total investment in 1973 to 24% in 1981. It accounted for 48% of the GDP in 1981–82.[4]

It is interesting to look at the sectoral composition of the stimulated private investments as between the plan period that has just ended and the current plan period (see Table 1).

The Open Door Policy involved a variety of administrative and legislative measures. Law No. 43 of 1974 concerning the Investment of Arab and Foreign Funds and the Free Zones, as amended by Law No. 32 of 1977, states that "projects may not be nationalised or confiscated ... except by judicial procedures" (Article 7) and offers the enterprises several privileges and exemptions.

The companies coming under this law are deemed to belong to the private sector; and legislation and regulations applicable to the public sector do not apply to them. For example, the conditions and procedures for electing labour representatives to the boards of directors of public sector enterprises etc. do not apply to them except that the companies' own statutes shall provide for labour participation in management by some method (Article 10). Employees and board members are exempted from the provisions of Law No. 113 of 1961 that limits remunerations (Article 11).

TABLE 1

PRIVATE INVESTMENT IN EGYPT

Sector	Private investment as % of total investment	
(1)	1977–82 Plan Period (2)	1982–87 Plan Period (3)
Agriculture and land reform, irrigation and drainage	29	27
Industry and metallurgy	23	21
Petroleum	–	–
Electricity	–	–
Contracting	24	54
Total Commodity Sector	20	20
Transport and Communication	3	6
Suez Canal	–	–
Commerce, finance, insurance and tourism	14	33
Total production service section	5	8
Housing	74	94
Public Utilities	–	–
Education, Health, other services	16	26
Total Service Sector	36	45
Total fixed investments	20	23

Source: *The Five Year Plan's Development Pillars and Policies 1982/83–1986/87, p. 63.*

Besides, the projects of the enterprises are exempted from a variety of taxes (under Articles 16 and 17). It is interesting to note that under Article 6 enterprises established "entirely with Egyptian capital and owned by Egyptian nationals" also enjoy many of the above-cited privileges. Joint ventures involving foreign capital can be so organised as to allow "majority foreign ownership and management control," with one exception, viz. banks, where the Egyptian share should be at least 51%.[5]

There have been other elements of privatisation in government policies. As regards the enterprises that stay in the public sector – and these will be a very large number indeed – the government has evolved new policies in two important directions. First, the managers are provided with a greater degree of autonomy than before.[6] Second, the government has determined that there was "no alternative" to a careful cost-benefit analysis of every project, to ensuring efficient implementation of investment at the lowest costs possible, to the choice of efficient technical and management systems, and to the reducing of losses at every stage of the production process. The Plan document (1982–87) is replete with such desiderata as "reconsidering the management of the public sector to raise its productivity," reducing subsidies, and fixing prices "on economic basis," and "fixing a remunerative price that ensures a reasonable rate of profit enough to finance investment."[7]

B. SUDAN

The Sudanese case reinforces the theme of rethinking traced in the experience of Egypt. At several points we have evidence that supports the conceptual variations in the theme outlined in the opening section of this paper.

Policies progressively favouring or encouraging private investment have had the effect of raising such investment from 39% of the total investment in 1955–61 to 58% in 1968–72. The 1978–83 Plan mentioned among the objectives "encouraging the private sector, both foreign and local, to play its role fully and effectively in development."[8] Many incentives[9] have been offered to private investment – "national capital" as well as foreign capital. For instance, exemptions have been granted from business profits tax for up to five years, and from export duties. Land is made available at reduced prices; and electricity and transport rates are reduced. Customs duties may be increased on the imports of commodities which compete with, or which are substitutes for, the products of the projects concerned; or the imports may be restricted for a period. Guarantee is given against nationalisation "unless the public good so requires and by virtue of a law." But in any such case fair compensation is contemplated after evaluation of property at the prices current at the time of nationalisation. The evaluation as well as any remittances abroad will be promptly made.

Further, the Consultative Committee set up under the Encouragement of Investment Act will include four members from the private sector.

Apart from the incentives to private investment, government policies reflect close attention to several substantive elements of privatisation.

Let us look at the organisational measures first. Public holding companies in the sugar, textile and cement sectors were abolished. This, it is claimed, has led to an enhancement in the autonomy of the operating plants and must have promoted some degree of healthy competition.

Next, financial criteria of public enterprise operations have been significantly marketised. For instance, prices have been revised so as to offer "incentives to production."[10] Several subsidies were eliminated. Financial arrangements within the irrigated agriculture sector have been completely restructured and the minimum level of revenues that the Egyptian banks should generate was agreed with the International Monetary Fund in 1982. And, on the whole, a conscious attempt has been made to strengthen the finances of the public enterprise sector.

Further, the emphasis currently placed on the use of limited resources to rehabilitate existing production potential, rather than for new projects,[11] illustrates the shift in thinking in favour of maximising the returns of investment or a trend towards some degree of marketisation of the economy.

C. ETHIOPIA[12]

The Ethiopian case brings out but one point, viz., that a government almost committed to total nationalisation of the industrial economy, has begun to appreciate the need for the introduction of foreign capital, which can be private in nature. The modality is that of a joint venture, in which the foreign shareholding shall not ordinarily exceed 49%. The participation is between foreign capital and Ethiopian public capital only and is intended to offer Ethiopia the benefits of foreign technology.[13] The foreign investor is offered incentives of certain tax exemptions and protection of "the right of ownership" of shares. In the event of the government buying all the shares for reasons of national interest, a "fair and equitable price" will be paid. A close study of the legislation concerned indicates, however, that the joint venture can be exposed to the characteristics of a public enterprise whose directoral and decision making is vested predominantly in the hands of the majority shareholder, viz. the Government.

D. KENYA

The current trends of thought on the relative role of public enterprises in Kenya provide rich evidence on the multifarious modalities of privatisation analytically presented in the opening section.

The economic policies of Kenya have originated from the concept of African socialism enunciated in 1965, which envisaged that "the power to control resource use resides with the State." It would be an "error of great magnitude," however, to assume that this could be achieved only through ownership.[14]

Kenya has been a mixed economy and the question of what enterprises to nationalise or sponsor in the public sector has always been dealt with in a pragmatic manner. The 1965 paper on African socialism upheld as a critical issue: "under what circumstances and decision making is vested predominantly in the hands of the majority shareholder, viz., the Government.

Nationalisation will be needed:

(i)   when the assets in private hands threaten the security or undermine the integrity of the nation; or
(ii) when the production resources are being wasted; or
(iii) when the operation of an industry by private concerns has a serious detrimental effect on the public interest; or
(iv) when other less costly means of control are not available or are not effective."[15]

It would be relevant to our theme to excerpt from the paper the following, almost conclusive, observation:

> Nationalisation ... will be considered if the need is urgent, if other less costly controls are ineffective, and if it is understood that most industries nationalised will not be operated at a loss.[16]

The number of public enterprises of one kind or another has

increased colossally over the years. A recent count on government investments revealed the following data.[17]

Total number of statutory boards			147
Companies:			
(a) wholly owned by the government		47	
(b) in which the government has controlling interest		36	
(c) in which the government/ statutory boards have minority interest		93	176
Total Government involvement			323

The sectoral spread of public enterprise has been very wide. Working from published data,[18] we can present the following cross-classification as between sizes of public sector industries and the public shares in those industry categories (Table 2). The boxes on the top left represent public sector activities which are small in aggregate size and which account for small proportions of employment in those industries in the country; while the boxes on the bottom right refer to industries of large absolute size in the public sector, which constitute a major part of the concerned activities in the country. There is a wide spread in between these extremes. On the whole, most of the industries which attracted relatively small governmental involvement are of relatively small size within the public sector; while the large public sector industries account for high degrees of the concerned activities in Kenya. To put this in another way, (large) public enterprises enjoy significant degrees of monopoly power; and several small public enterprise activities exist which are exposed to competition from the private sector.

Kenyan public enterprises have a complex ownership structure. Some are wholly owned by the government; some are wholly owned by the government and public enterprises; some are wholly owned by public enterprises and, in some cases, jointly with private investors; and some in all these categories are majority owned and some others are minority owned by the government and/or public enterprises. Interesting investment relationships exist, under which a major public enterprise and one of its subsidiaries hold shares in an enterprise (which thus becomes a subsidiary of both of them); in some cases the public ownership, even if minority, is diffused over several enterprises. It is not our purpose to explain these facts – some are just historical in significance; but it may be relevant to note these, as the next, analytical section, bears out.

One other point of fact worth noting is that public enterprises are found in almost all sectoral categories – heavy, basic, infrastructural, light, manufacturing, finance and services. Today the government has ownership interest in textiles, shoes, sugar, tyres, alcohol, pharmaceuticals, canning, mining, salt, drilling, paper, hotels, cement, batteries, vehicles, radios, fishing, engineering, beverages and food processing.[19] And public investments constitute a "very sizeable proportion of the total capital formation in the country."[20] Working on the data found in the Statistical Abstract (Table 3), we can deduce a clear trend of increase in the relative contribution of the public enterprise sector to capital formation, sector by sector and on the whole.[21]

Let us pursue the trends of rethinking on the role and extent of public enterprise in Kenya. The Ndegwa Committee (1979), in the course of an intensive review of the public enterprise situation, observed that the growth in this sector "has not been accompanied by development of efficient management systems to ensure that the sector plays its role in an efficient manner." They were struck by "clear evidence," in many cases, of "prolonged inefficiency, financial mismanagement, waste and malpractices." They feared "the danger of over-politicising production and production through the establishment of too many parastatals." They felt that "certain existing organisations ought to be abolished." It was evident to them that many public enterprises "have deviated from their primary functions." They concluded that the shortcomings they discovered constituted "a serious threat to the economy."

It is interesting to refer to the Committee's emphatic observation, in 1979, that "the economic and social costs of delay in taking action" to remedy the serious problems of the public enterprise sector "are simply unacceptable." The trend of introspection continued and got concretised into positive thought in favour of "divestiture" when the Working Party on Government Expenditures reviewed the situation in 1982. The Working Party opined that most of the public investments "are not strategic in any sense of the word," and that "government participation in commercial enterprise has been carried well beyond original con-

TABLE 2

SIZE AND MONOPOLY IN THE PUBLIC ENTERPRISE SECTOR (KENYA)

No. of wage employees in the public sector industry	% of public sector wage employment in the total in the industry					
	Below 10	10–25	25–50	50–75	75–100	100
Below 100	Drugs and medicines Wholesale trade Retail butcheries Oil and petrol retail General retail Ocean and Coastal transport Services incidental to transport Storage and warehousing "Other" insurance Property companies	Mining & quarrying				
100–200	Metal products Electrical contractors Food – wholesale trade "Other" passenger transport	Soft drinks			Pottery	Pipelines

200–500	"Other" agricultural activities General wholesale trade Freight by road	Engineering products: wholesale trade	Cotton ginneries Accounting etc.			Petroleum refining
500–1,000	Hotels etc.	Grain mills Printing etc.	Insurance companies	Ship building and repairing	Chemical and fertilizer Mineral mining Manufacture & repair of aircraft Financial services	Inland water transport K.P. & T administrative services
1,000–2,000		Spinning, weaving and finished textiles	Manufacture & assembly of motor vehicles	Slaughtering, etc. Basic chemicals Cement Painters, roof tiles etc. in construction "Other" financial institutions		KR Central
2,000–5,000		Ranches	Agricultural products: wholesale trade Air transport Monetary institutions		Supporting services to air transport communications	Electricity Railways
5,000–10,000		Mixed farming	Food products (manufacturing)	Sugar	Water	
10,000–and above				Sugar plantations "Other" construction (not building)	Agricultural services	Forestry Railroad equipment Supporting services to water transport

Source: Basic data taken from: *Statistical Abstracts 1981*, Central Bureau of Statistics. (November, 1982), pp. 240–4.

TABLE 3

CONTRIBUTION OF THE PUBLIC ENTERPRISE SECTOR TO CAPITAL
FORMATION, BY INDUSTRY (1979) (AS PERCENTAGE OF TOTAL)

Sector (1)	1964 (2)	1970 (3)	Percentage 1979 (4)
Agriculture	7.6	4.1	11.2
Forestry	100.0	100.0	100.0
Fishing	–	–	–
Mining and quarrying	–	90.8	–
Manufacturing	2.7	36.7	27.2
Building and construction	18.2	14.2	11.1
Electricity and water	17.6	90.3	100.0
Transport, storage and communications	39.7	46.6	64.8
Wholesale, retail trade, restaurant and hotels	7.8	9.7	9.5
Finance, insurance, real estate and business services	7.8	16.3	57.6
Ownership of dwellings	51.1	42.4	52.5
Other services	1.8	0.4	5.8
Total	20.1	35.8	38.1

Source: *Statistical Abstracts*, volumes for 1970, 1975 and 1979 (Nairobi).

ceptions." They recommended it as a "matter of high priority for the government to revise this trend by working out a viable programme for divesting itself of some of its investments to Kenyan investors."

The privatisation plan, envisaged by the Working Party, is multi-pronged and calls for distinguishing public enterprises among four categories:

(i) those whose retention as government agencies or enterprises is essential to accelerated and equitable national development and the regulation of the private sector;
(ii) those whose objectives have been achieved and which should be discontinued;
(iii) those whose functions could be absorbed by parent–ministries; and

(iv) those whose functions would be more efficiently performed
by the private sector.

That the government's own thinking was on similar lines may be
inferred from the Sessional Paper on Development Prospects and
Policies (1982) which spoke of "the return" of some public enterprises "to private sector operation."[22]

The recommendations of the Working Party met with government approval. The President of Kenya was convinced that "a
number of these public enterprises could be made more productive and more profitable in the hands of private Kenyans as
owners and managers."[23] In June 1983, he appointed a Task Force
on Divestiture of Government Investment, as recommended by
the Working Party, with the following terms of reference:

(1) To carry out a careful review of the parastatal sector and come
    out with two distinct groups of parastatals, namely those
    which are public oriented and which provide public goods
    and services, and those which are private sector oriented.

(2) To study the legal, financial and organisational character-
    istics of parastatals and determine:

    (a) those in which Government involvement, direct or in-
         direct, should be reduced or terminated.
    (b) those whose functions can be absorbed by the parent
         Ministries or other parastatals.
    (c) those which require legal, functional, financial and or-
         ganisational re-adjustment or restructuring.
    (d) methods and strategies of implementing recommenda-
         tions on items 2(a)–(c) above.

(3) To study the existing capital market and recommend effec-
    tive strategies and appropriate mechanisms through which
    the Government should dispose of its investments.

The Task Force has been at work which, undoubtedly, has
complex dimensions.

3

Why Privatisation?

Let us take a critical look at the factors that may have prompted thought in favour of some kind and degree of privatisation in the African countries, particularly those covered by the preceding section. (We keep aside any sudden emergence of rightist ideology, which is, in fact, untrue in the cases covered.)

Figure 2 presents an overall view of the argument contained in this section.

A. MACRO FACTORS

(1) The first of these refers essentially to the government's decision to attract foreign capital so as to avail of the technology and the investment opportunities that it provides. In the process the overall proportion of private holding in the economy might increase, assuming that the foreign capital is private. This is about the major sense in which privatisation can be spoken of with reference to Ethiopia.

(2) An interesting connection between macro investment needs and privatisation can be derived from the Egyptian experience. For a time the private sector, whose savings "went up enormously," did not find "open doors to absorb its savings capacity" and therefore moved towards increased consumption or speculation or investment abroad. This, the government realised, was a lost opportunity. There could be ways of catching private savings for public investment, but it was felt that they might have a "high cost if required for government investment."[24]

A similar trend of thought is perceptible at the governmental levels in Kenya – an openly mixed economy. Fixed capital formation in the private sector fell seriously from 1979 to 1982. Government borrowings from the banking system led to a curtailment of lending to the rest of the economy. The President ob-

FIGURE 2

THE RATIONALE OF PRIVATISATION

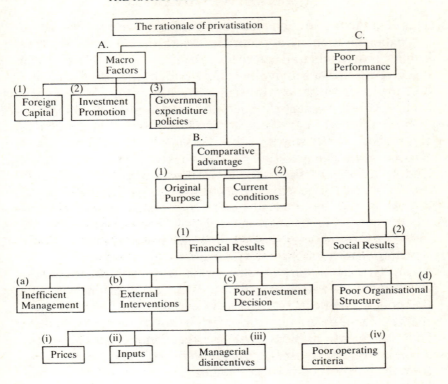

served that "the private sector requires more funds and these can only be obtained if Government borrows and spends less."[25]

(3)   Closely related to the preceding consideration is the compulsion experienced by many governments to curtail public expenditures as a matter of overall economic and budgeting policy. Agreements with IMF have often included limitations on government expenditures – as in Sudan;[26] and expenditure ceilings have been set for each ministry in Kenya, which correspondingly restrict the room for government investments in public enterprises. The area open for private investment, including foreign capital not borrowed or guaranteed necessarily by the government, expands in such a situation.

B. COMPARATIVE ADVANTAGE

This ought to be the main plank on which the case for privatisation (or nationalisation in appropriate cases) should rest. What is implied is that, when an enterprise loses its comparative advantage in a given sector of activity by being a public enterprise, there is a case for its privatisation (in whatever sense).[27]

(1) An easy segment under this head is that of enterprises "whose objectives have been achieved and which should be discontinued," in the words of the Working Party on Government Expenditures (Kenya, 1982).[28] Units taken over when sick are eligible to privatisation once the sickness is cured. Such easy examples apart, two difficult problems need to be added in the context of the "original purpose:" how easy is it to determine whether it is achieved; more basically, is the original purpose valid today? Solutions are, no doubt, easier in a mixed economy than in a predominantly public-enterprise oriented economy.

(2) Gradual diminutions in market imperfections weaken the comparative advantages of public enterprises. It is from this angle that policy statements such as Ivory Coast's should be appreciated: that there will be gradual relaxations in government intervention and investment.[29] Besides, changes in economic strategy can have a bearing on the scope for privatisation. This may be evidenced from the current conditions of Sudan. The emphasis of the Three Year Public Investment Programme is on fuller utilisation and rehabilitation of existing plant.

C. POOR PERFORMANCE

The most powerful factor underlying thoughts favouring some privatisation seems to lie in the poor results recorded by public enterprises across the board. These have to be considered strictly under two heads – financial and social; and a balanced view has to be taken on performance.

Let us look at the social returns first. These, in a sense, provide the major justification for a public enterprise. For one to conclude that it has no case on this ground one has to (i) be certain of what the social returns under review are and (ii) be able to demonstrate that the social returns realised are outweighed by the lowness of the financial results. Not only are these determinations difficult at the technical level but they are bound to be unlikely on political grounds. We do not have much evidence under this head, except for such a finding by the Working Party in Kenya (in 1982) that government joint ventures have, in some cases, led to "some de-Kenyanisation of the economy."[30]

For a stimulus for privatisation on the ground of results, we have, therefore, to concentrate on the financial returns.

Here the evidence is ubiquitous. The returns are so poor that, despite valid notions of social benefits, governments have become seriously concerned. The Working Party (in Kenya) produced some figures to indicate that the Government was receiving very low returns on an investment of about K£900 million. Data on the Sudanese public enterprises merited the official pronouncement that "their net contribution to domestic capital formation has been minimal."[31] Enterprises in many sectors – industrial and agricultural – made serious losses (in 1978–79).[32] And their indebtedness to the Bank of Sudan increased considerably between 1979 and 1981.[33] The Plan document of Egypt (1982–83) emphasises: "there is no alternative ... to reducing losses in every stage of production" and commends the fixing of a "remunerative price that ensures a reasonable rate of profit enough to finance investment."[34]

While poor financial results have begun to set governments thinking on the role and performance of public enterprises, it is difficult to expect privatisation in the sense of denationalisation as a quick solution. Three sets of reasons exist. First, it is difficult on political and ideological grounds. Second, the deficits of some public enterprises are planned deficits – for social reasons; hence deficits are not a conclusive ground for denationalisation. Third, many of the enterprises can improve in net financial position if, irrespective of ownership, operating criteria were rationalised. It is in the last sense that privatisation has significance – even in public–enterprise oriented (or socialist) economies. We have already noted certain structural operating and managerial changes initiated in Egypt and Sudan.

The precise processes of privatisation in this sense call for an accurate classification of the causes of deficits; for the direction of privatisation varies with the cause. Inefficient management must prompt measures of marketisation of managerial hiring and incentives and of arrangements of private participation through joint ventures. External interventions are of two kinds. We have to live with the socially desirable ones; the other kind ought to be curbed. Progress in privatisation of ownership can help in this. But whether politicians are keen on such a result is doubtful. A major direction of privatisation which can exorcise the problem consists of the evolution of operating criteria that bring the enterprise management close to market discipline, once the socially desired interventions are provided for. This seems to be the trend of enterprise reforms in countries like Egypt where "the public sector continued as a pioneer in development during the last two decades, this will continue in the future";[35] and in Sudan, where significant structural changes costing holding company structures and monopoly power, despite public ownership, are being implemented. In a clearly mixed economy such as the Kenyan, on the other hand, both structural adjustments within public ownership and denationalisation are possible, as is implicit in the government pronouncement that "structural adjustment must embrace a more constructive and profitable role for essential parastatals and the return of others to private sector operation."[36]

The second term of reference set for the Task Force on Divestiture[37] (in Kenya) suggests the scope of options within the principle of privatisation.

In concluding this section, it may be reiterated that the most valid ground on which to think of privatisation is the loss of comparative advantage on the part of a public enterprise and not just financial deficits, though the latter have, in many cases, triggered thought in this area.

One financial illustration of the changing trends of thought on the role of public enterprise in the national economy may be drawn from the current Development Plan of Nigeria:

> Public sector investment will continue to complement private investment and be largely confined to areas where private initiative has failed to respond or responded too slowly to meet the demands of the economy. Such investment, will, however, as much as possible, be undertaken *in co-operation with private interests*. This is to ensure that such government ventures are run along commercial lines rather than as social services. Every public venture will be expected to pay its way

even if, for social reasons, it is considered undesirable to insist on profit maximisation. Apart from the defence industries and security printing, no specific area will be reserved exclusively for government.[38]

4

Problems of Privatisation

Privatisation is not as easy as it sounds. The nature of problems varies from country to country and depends on the precise direction in which any of the available options under that generic policy is adopted (see Section 1). We shall highlight the major issues that call for attention and control on the African scene.

(a)   Let us consider, first, the denationalisation of an enterprise and comment on the sale price.

If it has been in deficits, it may not prove easy to sell it to private investors except at prices low enough to attract them. How low should they be? Assuming that the shares of the enterprise are not quoted on the stock exchange, we are short of that kind of guidance. Whether it should be sold for a price that equals the net capital worth (i.e. original investment minus accumulated deficits) has no quick answer for the following reasons: (i) the figure of accumulated deficits is the product of accounting practices of past years concerning the treatment of costs. One cannot be certain that it represents all, or only those, costs that ought to have been charged to current operations year after year so far. (ii) That figure and therefore the net worth computation correspond to current operating profitability arising from the existing managerial structures, criteria and practices. It is possible that changes in these, which could not be effected while the enterprise has been in the public sector, can easily be effected on denationalisation and can then cause a sudden increase in profitability. The present worth basis might therefore amount to an understatement of the real worth of the enterprise in the hands of the new investors.

In the circumstances of the capital markets prevailing in most African countries and by virtue of certain considerations restrictive of buyer potential (see later paragraphs in this section), the denationalisation may smack of a distress sale. Add to this proneness to bargaining skills or irregularities; the inconclusiveness of the price is all the more certain and the economics as well as the

ethics of the measure may fall into the area of doubt and con-
troversy.

A useful guideline in this context would be that, where ame-
liorative steps are possible in restructuring the capital, production
and management structures, these should be implemented prior to
putting the enterprise on sale. It is to be appreciated that the
Kenyan policy comprehends making currently unprofitable enterprises profitable "before the disposition of shares,"[39] wherever
possible.

Turning to a profitable enterprise marked out for denationalisation on grounds of comparative advantage, we encounter a
price problem of another kind. Do the accounts reflect its true
value? Here one has to look at the implications of inflation. It is
unlikely that in the state of accounting sophistication generally
prevalent in the African countries the assets are appropriately
revalued. So the capital worth, exclusive of revaluation reserves,
turns out to be lower than the real worth of the enterprise. Add to
this that the potential buyers are smart people; the sale price may
prove artificially low.

An important requirement of a smooth policy of government
disinvestment is to provide for a system of price determination, as
opposed to ad hoc decisions. Some form of an independent commission may be entrusted with this function, on the basis of
guidelines from the government. An interesting example, drawn
from a like context, is the Capital Issues Commission set up in
Nigeria to determine the prices at which "alien enterprises or
shares of alien enterprises" are to be sold or transferred to the
nationals, under the Nigerian Enterprises Promotion Decree
(1977).

(b)   There is an important implication of privatisation which
goes beyond the narrow context of public enterprise. It concerns
the distributional effects and has particular relevance in the African region. For (i) the income and wealth disparities are high;
(ii) the development plans, almost everywhere, have emphasised
reductions in such disparities as a major objective;[40] (iii) the "elite"
groups that can knock off the divested assets are already rich; and
(iv) domestic capital potential is relatively low. The question,
therefore, assumes significance: who buys the divestments?

It would be of interest to classify the groups of potential investors as follows:

(i)   African nationals
(ii) Nationals of non-African origin and
(iii) Foreigners

The first would be the most welcome group, if only it were large enough. But consequences of concentration can easily unleash themselves. It may therefore be appropriate for governments to consider the desirability of regulating the size of ownership of the divestitures per capita or in any other way. (Precedent is not wanting in this direction of policy. Nigeria has legislated certain provisions intended to limit individual purchase of "alien shares of firms" with the object of minimising economic concentration through that channel.)[41] Two questions remain, however: what practical effect such regulations have, and whether they defeat the major aim of divesting government investments in enterprises.

These questions acquire special force when we come to the second group, for they introduce the ethnic dimension. It is difficult to dilate on what impact this will have in practice, though the possibility of its weakening the implementation of denationalisation measures can be real from time to time.

The third group raises a different problem, namely, the degree of foreign control over the national economy. To the extent that it can be under the effective influence of the government, as in a joint venture in which the public shareholding is major, vide the Egyptian and the Ethiopian laws on the subject, the danger may not be serious. But there is already evidence in some countries like Kenya, where, in some cases, the practice of joint ventures has had undesirable effects.[42] It has to be recognised that the policies of privatisation, for the best results, have to be accompanied by suitable measures of effective public watchfulness on the working of foreign capital holdings either in partnership with the government or with local private capital or on their own. The case for such measures is indeed independent of privatisation policies, but the best results of the latter for the national economy flow from them. This conclusion has extensive validity; it applies not only to the sale of a divestment (or positive denationalisation) but also to the admission of private capital in a joint venture with the government in an existing or a new enterprise or into an activity without public or any other local equity participation whatsoever.

(c)   Privatisation might lead to certain changes in the pattern of public enterprise and ownership. Assume that the indigenous nationals are not capable of taking over the investments that the government divests itself of but that the government is anxious that the ownership of the divested shares or enterprises should not go to "others." It is just probable that it initiates a financial mechanism in the public sector for advancing funds to the local people so as to enable them to bid for the divestments as evidenced by Nigerian experience in indigenising alien investments. On certain conditions of course; probably on the show of some resource potential on their own part. The net outcome can well be that, while the government disinvests certain of its investments in production units, its investments in enterprises that finance potential investors increase somewhat. Privatisation thus does not eventually imply a net reduction in governmental or public investments equivalent to the initial divestments. On occasions this can prove to be a problematic trend; for, the government's stake is now proportional, not to the potentialities of production units, but to the repaying capability and/or willingness of the local borrowers. It is not too rarely that the latter has been found to be low.

Another aspect of change in the entrepreneurial character of public enterprise that remains after privatisation measures are introduced is that, by and large, the relatively profitable enterprises, the quick-yielding projects, and the downstream activities get transferred to the private sector; whereas the more basic ones and those that are likely to make low profits or deficits for social reasons stay put in the public sector. There is nothing intrinsically wrong in this, provided that the financial character of these enterprises is the result of conscious decision on social grounds. Yet two consequences follow. First, the situation contributes to budgetary difficulties in the sense that the current flow as between the public exchequer and the public enterprise sector turns out to be unfavourable to the former. This may lead to additional taxation or deficit financing of any budgetary gap. Though such an event flows directly from the government's decision to subsidise certain activities, the impression it generates all round is that because of privatisation the government is hard put to resort to it. The fear of such criticism can operate against further measures of privatisation, though the case for the latter may in fact be intrinsic, on grounds of comparative advantage.

The second is a more material consequence in terms of substance. The net outcome of privatisation measures that retain losses in the public sector and shift profits to the private sector will be a distributional inequity, especially in the circumstances of a least developed country characterised by wide income disparities. The African scene, as a cross-section, comes within this description. The fruits of profitable activities rest with private investors – the fewer, the less dispersed the shareholding; while the impacts of budget deficit begin to be reflected in (probably) regressive tax measures. Public resentment may build up slowly but surely against such trends, the more certainly when the profits of the privatised units have been built on the edifice of gestation losses squarely borne by the public sector in the pre-privatised days. Other things being equal, social tempers may rise with a vengeance in favour of renationalisation measures as time goes on. It is best to avoid such causes of instability in policy, by designing orderly strategies of privatisation. In other words, privatisation should be a channel for productive efficiency and surplus generation but not an unlimited gift of easy profit to private investors.

(d) Privatisation has two fundamental implications in the context of planned development which happens to be the strategy of most African countries. The first concerns the sectoral areas and production functions, in respect of which privatised or private units are not under the same discipline of priorities as apply to public sector investments. There is need then for helpful, if not effective, guidelines from the government – a point clearly re-cognised in the current Plan document of Egypt. It is equally important that in the least developed countries of Africa the competence of private investors, on an average, in project for-mulation and operational strategies is not as high as one should deem necessary. This is in fact an original reason for the emer-gence of the public enterprise sector. It is therefore desirable for the government to promote specialist technical services under public aegis, which can provide the needed expertise to private investors. Once again, current Egyptian planning recognises this need.

The other implication is related to the basic conflict between the interests of growth and distributional justice. Privatisation meas-ures are largely a product of pro-growth considerations. Yet, as suggested at several places in this section, privatisation leads to some concentration and some aggravation of income and wealth disparities. The latter may be considered as a cost in achieving growth. How far such a cost is acceptable to the nation depends on its social ideology, development status and current state of public finances. There can be no generalisation by way of an answer. What is important to note is that some conscious answer is essential, so that the government can go ahead with the smooth implementation of a policy of privatisation that it opts for. Or else, practice becomes so inconsistent and ad hoc that the eventual results may turn out to be insubstantial.

NOTES

1. *Part One – The Present – The 5-Year Plan's Development Pillars and Policies* 1982/83–1986/87 (Cairo), p. 32.
2. Law 43 of 1974 concerning the Investment of Arab and Foreign Funds and the Free Zones, as amended by Law No. 32 of 1977, Article 9 (Cairo, 1977).
3. See Article 10 of the above-cited Law of Egypt.
4. *Part One – The Present – The 5-Year Plan's Development Pillars and Policies: 1982/83–1986/87* (Cairo), p. 32.
5. Citi Bank, *Investment Guide* (Egypt), p. 23.
6. Heba Handoussa refers to the measures of decentralisation in control over public enterprises with the abolition of the General Organisations, which were analogous to holding companies, and to the granting of some autonomy to managers in the areas of employment, wage payments and pricing. "The impact of economic liberation on the performance of Egypt's public sector industry," Second BAPEG Conference, Boston 1980.
7. The Plan document already cited, pp. 23–7.
8. *The Six-Year Plan of Economic and Social Development – 1978/79–1982/83 V of 1* (Khartoum, 1977), p. 31.
9. *The Encouragement of Investment Act 1980* (Khartoum).
10. *Ministry of Finance and Economic Planning, Information Memorandum*, March 1983 (Khartoum, 1983), pp. 4–5.
11. Ibid., p. 6.
12. Somalia is another socialist country which practised large-scale nationalisation in the seventies and which has recently been offering a role to private enterprise in economic development. The Minister of Finance observed at the Industrial and Management Conference held in Mogadishu in October 1982 that "we would like to see it grow at least to the level of the public sector." And the Private Sector Department of the Ministry of Industry has recently been "strengthened." (*Industrial Management Review* (Mogadishu, Nov. 1983), pp. 14 and 16.)
13. *A Joint Proclamation to provide for the establishment of joint venture* (Negarit Gazeta, Addis Ababa, 22 Jan. 1983).
14. *African Socialism and its Application to Planning in Kenya* (Nairobi, 1965), p. 11.
15. Ibid., p. 27.
16. Ibid., p. 27.
17. *Report and Recommendations of the Working Party on Government Expenditures* (Nairobi, 1982), p. 92.
18. Central Bureau of Statistics, Ministry of Economic Planning and Development,

Statistical Abstract 1981 (Nairobi, 1982), pp. 240–4.

19. *Working Party on Government Expenditures*, op.cit., p. 42.
20. *Review of Statutory Boards*, Report and Recommendations of the Committee (Nairobi, 1979), p. 22.
21. *Statistical Abstracts*, pp. 39 and 36 of 1970 volume, pp. 49, 51 of 1975 volume and pp. 47 and 49 of 1979 volume.
22. Sessional Paper No. 4 of 1982 on *Development Prospects and Policies* (Nairobi, 1982), p. 14.
23. *Kenyatta Day: Message to the Nation*, by President David T. Arap Moi, 20 Oct. 1982.
24. The Plan document of Egypt, earlier cited, pp. 97–8. Also in Somalia, the latest industrial development policy underlines the promotion of private entrepreneurship and investment, with the objective of diverting "sizeable private investment from the traditional sectors of real estate, commerce and transport to productive industrial activity." (*Industrial Management Review* (Mogadishu, Nov. 1983) p. 26.)
25. Statement by the President on *The Current Economic Situation in Kenya*, 21 Sept. 1982 (Nairobi).
26. Ministry of Finance and Economic Planning, *Information Memorandum*, March 1983 (Khartoum), p. 5.
27. For an elaborate discussion on this issue see V.V. Ramanadham, *The Nature of Public Enterprise*, Part II, Section 8 (London, 1984).
28. Op.cit., p. 43.
29. *L'Expérience Ivoirienne de Planification* (1970), p. 24.
30. Op.cit., p. 41.
31. *The Six-Year Plan*, op.cit., p. 31.
32. Ministry of Financial and National Economy, *Economic Survey* 1978–79 (Khartoum).
33. Bank of Sudan, *Twenty-Second Annual Report, 1981* (Khartoum, 1982), p. 90.
34. The Plan documents cited earlier (pp. 22–3, 27).
35. The Plan document cited earlier, p. 32.
36. Sessional Paper No. 4 of 1982 on *Development Prospects and Policies* (Nairobi, 1982), p. 14.
37. Op.cit.
38. *Fourth National Development Plan 1981–85*, Vol. 1 (Lagos, 1981), p. 142.
39. *Working party*, op. cit., p. 43.
40. For example, "more even distribution of income among individuals and socio-economic groups." *Fourth National Development–Plan 1981–85*, Vol. 1 (Lagos, 1981), p. 37.
41. Some of the provisions of the Nigerian Enterprises Promotion Decrees of 1977 are cited below, rather extensively in view of their relevance to our theme.

    "In respect of all businesses listed in Schedule 1 and all businesses listed in Schedules 2 and 3 which are being operated other than as public companies (i.e. proprietorships, partnerships or private companies), no sale or transfer of interest can be effected unless the terms of sale or transfer have been approved by the Board. Alien owners of such enterprises will be allowed to submit names of prospective buyers, but the Board reserves the right to reject or vary whatever submissions are made to it;

    In case of public companies the Allotment Committee of the Capital Issues Commission will be responsible for allotment of share, or stocks;

    Both the Nigerian Enterprises Promotion Board and the Allotment Committee will take steps to ensure that the beneficial ownership of enterprises or shares of enterprises which are being sold for the purposes of complying with the provisions of the Decree are as widely spread as possible and deliberate efforts would be made to prevent the concentration of ownership in a few hands.

Except in the case of owner–managers, no enterprise or the entire mandatory portion of shares of any enterprise affected by the Decree would be sold or transferred to a single individual, and in no case will a single individual be allowed to have control of more than one enterprise affected by the Decree.

Except in the case of owner-managers, the maximum interest that any Nigerian citizen or non-public sector association (whether corporate or non-corporate) could be allowed to acquire in any one enterprise will be limited to five per cent of the equity shares being offered for sale or N50,000 worth of shares, whichever is higher. Nigerians are advised to note that the five per cent or N50,000 maximum rule is not as restrictive as it seems. However, any Nigerian citizen or association already holding more than the five per cent or N50,000 permissible maximum will not qualify for any further allotments, but will not be forced to divest any of his or its current holdings;

In considering applications from Nigerians to buy enterprises or shares of enterprises affected by the Decree, the Nigerian Enterprises Promotion Board or the Allotment Committee, as the case may be, will take into account the existing interest or shareholdings of such applicants in the enterprise or shares being sold and in any other enterprise or shares of enterprises affected by the Decree. In this connection the Nigerian Enterprises Promotion Board or the Allotment Committee, as the case may be, is not obliged to approve in whole or in part, any application from any Nigerian citizen or association (whether corporate or non-corporate) for the purchase of enterprises or shares of enterprises affected by the Decree. Besides, the Board or the Allotment Committee reserves the power to request for any information whatsoever from any Nigerian citizen or association (whether corporate or not) seeking to purchase shares or interest in enterprises affected by the Decree;

All Schedules 2 and 3 enterprises as well as enterprises complying under Section 7(1) of the Decree, are obliged to reserve not less than 10 per cent of the amount of sale for their employees. At least one-half of the 10 per cent must also be reserved for the non-managerial staff. Any lawful arrangement under which the acquisition of the shares by workers will be achieved or facilitated will be favourably considered by the Board provided that the arrangement is not obnoxious. The Nigerian Enterprises Promotion Board is always ready to advise and assist enterprises to ensure that Government objective of worker equity participation is achieved".

42. *Working Party*, op.cit., p. 41. Also, David Wainaina Gachuki, "Public Enterprise and Foreign Capital in Kenya: The Policy Environment," in *The Role of Public Enterprises in Development in Eastern Africa*, co-ordinated by Hans G. Klaus and S.E. Migot-Adholla (Institute for Development Studies, Nairobi, 1980): "Government participation means that the investors hold it as a hostage against the government to extract concessions to certain privileges" (p. 208).

INDEX

References to tables are italicised